Stopping Your Self-Sabotage:
Steps to Increase Your Self-Confidence

By

Dr. Darryl Cross

By the same Author:

Available on www.amazon.com

Growing up Children: How To Get 5 – 12 Year Olds To Behave & Do As They're Told

Teenager Trouble-Shooting: How to Stop Your Adolescent Driving You Crazy

The Dark Clouds at Work: How to Manage Depressed Staff in the Workplace Whilst Increasing Morale and Productivity

Available on www.drdarryl.com

Listen Up Now! How to Increase Profit and Growth in Business by Really Listening to Your Clients & Customers

Cover design by Nu-Image Design

Published by Crossways Publishing

Copyright © 2010 by Darryl Cross. All rights reserved

Reproduction and distribution in any way shape, or form is forbidden. No part of this book shall be reproduced, stored in a retrieval system, or transmitted by any other means, electronic, mechanical, photocopying, recording, or otherwise, without prior written permission from the author.

ISBN-10: 0-9806101-1-7
ISBN-13: 978-0-9806101-1-6

Disclaimer

This publication is designed to provide accurate and authoritative information with regard to the subject matter covered. It is sold with the understanding that the author is not engaged in rendering legal, accounting or financial advice of any kind. If legal advice or other medical or professional assistance is required of any nature, the services of a competent professional in the appropriate area should be sought.

The author denies any liability for incidental or consequential damages resulting from the use of the information in this book. This book is designed to assist with generating and exploring various options for reducing and eliminating self-sabotage. It does not make decisions for the individual, but provides a range of options to be considered. No responsibility is accepted for any liabilities resulting from the actions of any parties involved.

CONTENTS

	Page
WELCOME	ix
CHAP. 1: THE MOST COMMON AFFLICTION	1
Chapter 1 Summary	9
CHAP. 2: SELF-SABOTAGE & INFERIORITY	11
Coping with Inferiority	24
Inferiority Feelings Are a Hallucination	26
How Do You Change Your Hallucination?	29
Chapter 2 Summary	30
CHAP. 3: UNDERSTANDING THE BASICS	31
Creatures of Habit	31
Thinking	34
Living Up to Your Potential	36
The Primary Emotion	37
Chapter 3 Summary	41
CHAP. 4: THE SILENT OPERATOR: YOUR SELF-TALK	43
Negative Thoughts	46
What Triggers Negative Self-Talk?	49
How Does Negative Self-Talk Work?	52
Chapter 4 Summary	58
CHAP. 5: THE PROCESS FOR POSITIVE SELF-TALK	59
What's the Process for Eliminating Self-Talk?	59
How Do You Actually Implement This Process in Daily Practice?	66
Chapter 5 Summary	70

CHAP. 6: SELF-TALK TRAPS FOR BEGINNERS   71
    Examples of Turning Negative Thoughts into
        Positive Thoughts   71
    Key Words and Phrases to Watch Out For   75
    Chapter 6 Summary   80

CHAP. 7: SELF-TALK QUESTIONS & ANSWERS   81
    Negative Questions   81
    Negative Statements   83
    Chapter 7 Summary   86

CHAP. 8: THE BOLD OPERATOR:
        YOUR SPOKEN WORD   87
    The Positive Spoken Word   89
    Chapter 8 Summary   92

CHAP. 9: THE VISUAL OPERATOR:
        YOUR SELF-PICTURE   95
    Mental and Physical Creations   95
    Visualize and It Happens   97
    Chapter 9 Summary   104

CHAP. 10: POSITIVE SELF-PICTURES   105
    Re-Imagine Yourself   105
    Positive Self-Pictures and Imagery   107
    Reprogramming Yourself   108
    Chapter 10 Summary   115

CHAP. 11: DISCIPLINE   117
    A "Dirty" Word   117
    Obstacles   120
    Make it Happen   126
    Chapter 11 Summary   130

Appendix - Thoughts Record Sheets   131
    A Blank One and a Completed Sample
About the Author   135

WELCOME

Welcome to this book which is a personal training program, designed to help you torpedo your self-sabotage and lift your self-confidence.

This book can also be used in conjunction with the Audio CD titled, *"I Want to be More Confident: How to Manage Your Self-Sabotage"* (visit the Store at www.drdarryl.com), in that it offers many of the aspects of this book in audio format so that you can listen at your leisure.

The strategies outlined in these pages have been refined over the last thirty-plus years of my work as a psychologist and coach. They work. They are the keys to success. Numerous clients of mine will tell you so. But there is a catch. **You have to make them work.** You have to be prepared to put in the effort. Do so and you'll see the rewards.

Are you ready to give it a go? Are you really prepared to invest energy and time in this? Are you up for this?

No doubt you are already one of those few who are seeking to better themselves, to grow and to personally develop. You probably wouldn't be reading this right now if you weren't concerned about growing and seeking to fulfill your potential and feel better about yourself.

Then, let's do it. This is essentially a 3-stage program that is broken down into a number of chapters to ensure that you master each step.

It is suggested that you read parts of this book as frequently as possible in order to absorb the lessons. Remember that "repetition is the mother of skill." Reading a part every day (even if it is just 10 minutes or so) keeps it "front of mind," as it were.

Of course, as in any training program, you will also be expected to do some exercises. This is how you make the principles stick. It's no good knowing about these principles; you need to be your own best friend and try them out. As I've often commented, *"Life rewards actions, not good intentions."*

Zig Ziglar once said, *"Too many people go to the grave with their music still in them."* It is my sincere hope therefore, that you will find your 'music' and grow and develop and be the person that you wish to be.

You owe it to yourself.

Darryl

CHAPTER 1

THE MOST COMMON AFFLICTION

What do you think is the most common issue that I have been asked in all my time of being a clinical and coaching psychologist? What is the one issue that people secretly ask about?

That's right. "How can I improve my self-confidence?" "How can I increase my self-esteem?" "How can I feel less shy?" "How can I feel less embarrassed?" "How can I be more outgoing?" Alternatively, I've had clients say things like, "I want to be more confident," "I want to be less self-conscious," "I want to be more assertive and not be afraid to say what I think," and finally, "I want to stop sabotaging myself."

Without any doubt at all, these have been the most commonly asked questions and the most common opening statements from clients throughout my whole career. These are the primary questions and issues. These are the questions and statements made by people of all ages, from both sexes, and from all cultures and communities.

However, there is another side to this whole issue. There is a flip-side. There are also those who present as "confident" and appear self-assured, but who come across as abrupt or curt, or perhaps seem arrogant or even aggressive, or who appear over-confident and maybe brash. They might appear confident, but they still sabotage themselves.

They come into my consulting room and ask,

- "How can I change my communication style?"
- "How can I communicate more effectively?"

Often they say things like,

- "My staff say I'm too aggressive."
- "My spouse tells me that I'm too domineering."
- "People tell me that I come across as arrogant."
- "People say that I'm sometimes gruff."

And then...maybe not straight away...comes the confiding comment that underneath it all, they feel under-confident, they lack confidence, they are really insecure.

Guess what?

Those who present as under-confident and those who present as arrogant, abrupt or over-confident typically have one thing in common – **they are both insecure!** They are both feeling inadequate and under-confident. They both sabotage themselves, but in different ways of course.

Ego is at the core of who we are. When the ego feels threatened or "not good enough," it goes into "fight or flight" mode, and becomes insecure and unsure, or over-compensates by being overly confident, even brusque, abrupt or arrogant. Sometimes, it becomes so insecure that it becomes a bully and dictatorial.

"Your mission is simple. You are asked to live so as to demonstrate that you are not an ego."

A Course in Miracles

None of us feel secure all of the time. Most of us feel insecure at times.

We all at some time or another, doubt ourselves or second-guess ourselves. That's only natural.

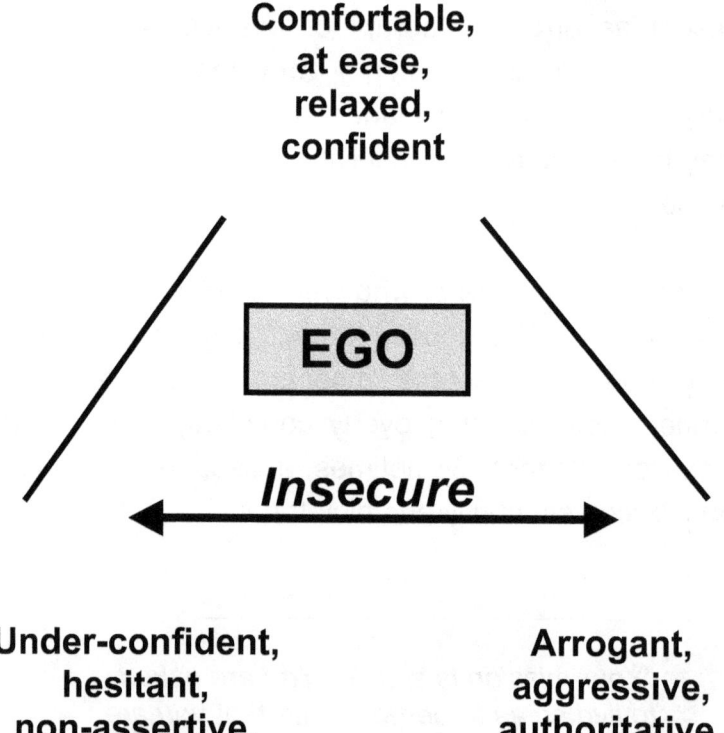

So, what would it mean to be confident, without feelings of inferiority or self-doubt and self-sabotage? It certainly needs to be said that over three decades of being a clinical psychologist and in the last ten years or more of being a coach, I have never met anyone who was always confident, 100% of the time.

Having said that, I definitely know individuals who are confident in themselves, who are "at home in their skin," who relate and connect meaningfully with those around them, and who have an inner belief in their ability to cope.

> *"It's not who you are that holds you back, it is who you think you are not."*
>
> Author Unknown

What does it feel like to be a confident person? What is the benchmark? What is the measure? To be confident means the following:

- to feel at ease with oneself
- to be self-assured
- to be able to rise above what others think of you
- to be able to relate and converse with a range of people, irrespective of culture, status or role
- to be free to give your opinion and perspective without fear of how you might be judged or evaluated
- to be able to express your emotions and thoughts openly
- to be generally relaxed and at home with yourself
- to know that you are your own person without having to compare yourself with others
- to allow others to be themselves without demanding that they meet particular expectations, and not to be controlling of others

- to be able to stand firm in the conviction of your own values and beliefs
- to take responsibility for your own actions and behavior without recourse to blame, fault-finding, or criticizing others
- to be able to move into unfamiliar situations knowing that somehow or other you can handle yourself appropriately
- to be able to see change as a challenge
- to be able to see past mistakes and learn from them without mourning the past or becoming stuck with "unfinished business" or regrets
- to be able to say "I'm sorry" without always apologizing or denigrating yourself
- to be able to take corrective action and coach yourself if a situation does not meet your expectations or specific needs, without unnecessarily beating up on yourself
- to be able to be internally supportive with positive self-talk
- to be content in your own company as well as content mixing and socializing with others
- to be able to give and receive love
- to feel happy with yourself

A long list?

Now, before you say that you'll never get to be all these things, this list is simply a guide as to what we are talking about in terms of self-confidence. Being confident is **not all** of these things. This is not indicative of the confident person all of the time, but this certainly typifies the person who could be said to be confident.

How would you like to be this kind of person? Is this the kind of person you aspire to be? Would you be proud of yourself to have achieved this level of personal competence, self-worth and understanding?

I think it's high time to address the issue of confidence and give it proper focus through a book and associated exercises that go beyond the four walls of my consulting room and beyond my telephone and email coaching.

What is it that I tell my clients in the confidentiality of my office or over the phone? What is it that means that they begin to achieve their goals, become the person they always dreamed of becoming, and feel confident in their ability to cope?

This book tells of those strategies that are given in private.

James was a friendly young man who said that he was 27 years of age, and that he realized that he had a life ahead of him, but he wasn't feeling successful, and felt that he was not going to make it given the struggles that he seemed to be having.

He lived alone but had previously coped by having a best friend with whom he did everything. It seemed that the two of them had become overly dependent on each other and almost enmeshed. However, life had all come to a head recently when James had become increasingly anxious at work, as well as in social settings, and things had overwhelmed him. He had confided to his aunt that he wasn't happy, and had broken down and cried. He knew that he needed help.

As we talked, James reported some tell-tale signs. He commented that he liked to get along with everyone (as we all do), didn't like conflict of any kind, and generally didn't stand up for himself. He also indicated that he liked to do a good job, but more than that, was very conscientious, didn't want to make any mistakes, and worked very hard to ensure that he got everything (yes everything) right.

When I suggested that it seemed like he was stuck with the internal "drivers," scripts or programs of "Pleasing Others" and "Being Perfect," he didn't object at all. He appeared relieved that at least he had a name for his struggles and why life seemed so difficult.

He now had an explanation for his self-sabotage.

Chapter 1 Summary

The most common psychological issue for the bulk of the population is improving or increasing their self-confidence. Even people who are seemingly confident on the outside are often insecure underneath.

Most of us feel insecure at times, inadequate and incompetent and when we do, we are sabotaging ourselves. We can improve ourselves through recognizing our self-sabotage and adopting new strategies to change our ways.

CHAPTER 2

SELF-SABOTAGE & INFERIORITY

It is now more common to hear the phrase *"self-sabotage."* Previously, people used to report that they suffered from what was generally called an *"inferiority complex."* Sometimes we hear people talk too about their *"limiting beliefs."* These terms have been used widely, but what do we mean by them? Are they the same? Essentially, the answer is "yes."

Typically, these people report that they feel they don't measure up, they feel inadequate, that somehow they fall short and are not meeting their standards or their goals. For example, they might be heard to say that they:

- lack confidence
- are embarrassed easily
- feel loath to speak up

- don't move out of their comfort zone
- detest public speaking
- feel awkward in groups and when meeting people
- are non-assertive with friends, employees or strangers
- feel anxious
- don't take risks
- are uncomfortable in social settings
- don't step out or try things
- lack courage
- have limiting self-beliefs
- are down on themselves
- feel that they let themselves down
- feel that they could achieve more

Alternatively, there are those who know that they are insecure, but seem to be expert at covering it up. (Sadly too, there are those who often don't know that they're insecure – but that's another story.) Those who do know and cover it up, usually know that deep down. However, they often get feedback from those around them that they:

- don't listen
- come across as arrogant
- seem to be abrupt or curt
- impose their own way on others
- ride rough-shod over others
- don't acknowledge others' feelings or opinions
- seem to be alone and isolated
- seem to not be really satisfied or happy

Russell was referred to me by his local doctor who had diagnosed clinical depression. His doctor had excused him from work and instructed him to visit a psychologist.

Russell was a national marketing manager for a well-known food company. He was 45 years old and had done a number of jobs, including being a consultant in his own business.

He sat across from me somewhat bewildered and confused, saying that he never in his wildest dreams would have expected to be sitting in front of a "shrink." He didn't quite know what on earth was going on with him and why he was feeling so badly.

He told me that he had only taken on his position 12 months previously, and that although he knew there were some issues that needed to be resolved, once he got into the job itself he realized that it was an "unholy mess."

Needless to say, he worked hard. Long hours. Huge workload. In the end, he wasn't able to turn the situation around and he became exhausted, de-motivated, and his work performance dropped off. His CEO recognized that he was struggling and looking poorly. Once he had been excused from work by his doctor, the company hired three people to do his job!

Russell said that he was probably just "burnt out" and needed a holiday.

> However, "burnt-out" and clinically depressed are not the same thing, and Russell was certainly presenting as depressed.
>
> So what was going on? We talked further.
>
> After some questioning, Russell confided that he'd never felt that he was up to the task in any job that he'd done; that he was never really good enough.
>
> In fact, he felt that he was really "a fake," and that someday "they" would all find out. Since he couldn't turn his current job around, it must be true – he was a fake and now they all knew!
>
> Now he and I understood the depression.
>
> The self-sabotage was clear. He believed his "stuff" about being a fake which incidentally, he'd picked up while still a young boy. It's enough to make anyone feel depressed!

EXERCISE 2.1:

Are there ways that you self-sabotage?
Times that you feel inferior?
Situations in which you don't measure up or have limiting beliefs?
Write them down here:

....

....

Self-Sabotage & Inferiority

....

....

....

....

Almost always, we consider that we are not good enough, not up to the mark somehow, or not performing in the way that we would like.

Interestingly, self-sabotage or inferiority is not something that clearly shows itself to others. Self-sabotage is not something that is immediately obvious to those around us.

An inferiority complex has nothing to do with the kind of lifestyle or possessions that show on the outside. **It has everything to do with what's on your inside** – the things you say to yourself in your head, the way that you limit yourself, and the things that you have typically learned from your family or those around you, especially when you were growing up.

Let's get one thing straight, though. You were **not** born inferior; you learned to be that way!

You did not arrive on the planet sabotaging yourself. You picked it up. As I have asked many of my clients: "Have you ever seen a baby arrive on the planet with an inferiority complex?" It just doesn't happen. We learn to feel inferior. We learn to sabotage ourselves. We learn limiting beliefs.

> **You were not born inferior. You learned to feel that way.**

For instance, people who self-sabotage or feel inferior generally have at least **one of the following *five* themes incorporated into their lives**. Do you do any of the following?

EXERCISE 2.2.1:

1. **Do you compare yourself with others?**
YES / NO

If Yes, on a Scale of 1 to 10, how often do you compare yourself with others, where 1 = Not at all and 10 = All the time?

What's your score? ....

We are good at comparing ourselves with those around us and seeing how we measure up. Certainly we can feel inferior if we think that we *should* be the same (or better) than others. This is one sure way to sabotage yourself.

For example, we say to ourselves things like,

> ➤ "I'm not as intelligent as…"
> ➤ "I wish I was as attractive as…"
> ➤ "I can't play sports like…"
> ➤ "I'm not as good as…"
> ➤ "I wish I was as rich as…"
> ➤ "Why can't I run a business like…"
> ➤ "I don't get promoted like all the others do."

We all have our own individual strengths and weaknesses. It is vital, therefore, to recognize our own strengths, focus on them, realize that we are good at some things and that we have some very worthwhile qualities (e.g., honesty, kindness, generosity).

As the saying goes: "Contentment is the reward that comes to those who feel that what they have is better than what they are missing."

EXERCISE 2.2.2 Continued:

2. Do you try to please others all (or most) of the time?   YES / NO

If Yes, on a Scale of 1 to 10, how often do you try to please others, where 1 = Not at all and 10 = All the time?

What's your score?   …………………

Somehow, some of us learn very early in life that in order to get along, to get rewards and to survive in the world, the best thing to do is to please other people. Get them to like us! Keep others happy by giving in to their needs, their wants and their desires. Then they'll like us and we'll be OK.

Take this to the extreme, however, and people end up pleasing others so much that they never (or rarely) end up pleasing themselves.

In a sense, they whittle themselves away. When people do this, they not only feel down and depressed, but they feel inadequate because they have successfully sabotaged themselves. They don't know who they really are because they have never allowed themselves the chance to consider themselves or to be their own person. ("What if they don't like me? That would be terrible.") They are lost to themselves. They don't know their strengths or talents and "what makes them tick". They haven't discovered what makes them unique, what makes them them!

"We'd be less concerned with what others thought of us if we knew how seldom they actually do."

Chinese Proverb

Certainly, it is fitting and appropriate to please others and help them, but to do so **all or most** of the time, to the continual detriment of yourself, is not wise. Continually pleasing others frequently means that you end up having nothing left for yourself. No time, no energy, nothing.

Starting to stand up for yourself and therefore having people say "no" to you might be the unthinkable. "Oh, how awful!" "How embarrassing." If someone says "no" to you, you take it personally. We don't like people to 'reject' us in any way.

What would happen if you started to consider your **own** needs and wants, your **own** feelings and thoughts?

Are you prepared to struggle with finding out who you really are? Finding out that you are a real person who does not have to rely on pleasing others all the time is freedom indeed.

"Why try to please everyone? The reality is that around 3 out of every 10 people are not going to like you anyway!"

Darryl Cross

When Sammy Davis Junior was on tour in Australia, he was asked, "What is the secret to success?" He replied, "I don't know, but what I do know is the secret to failure – it's trying to please everyone else."

EXERCISE 2.2.3 Continued:

3. Do you try to be perfect in all that you do?
                              YES / NO

If Yes, on a Scale of 1 to 10, how often do you try to be perfect, where 1 = Not at all and 10 = All the time?

What's your score? ....

Many people believe that if you feel inferior or second best, the way to handle it is to try to be perfect in what you do. If you do a really, really good job, you'll be accepted and others will like you. These perfectionists would hate to make a mistake or have someone criticize them. ("How dreadful." "How awful.")

They strive relentlessly for perfection but they always feel inferior because they never reach the perfection they want. It's never good enough. This is a dead-end. Certainly, too, it's rarely good enough for those around them who frequently find fault which just compounds the situation.

It's a no-win situation in which they have successfully sabotaged themselves. They try not to make mistakes and try hard to get things right all the time. They lack the spontaneity and freedom to experiment and be themselves. They experience real stress. They are under constant duress.

The message, instead, is that life is about making mistakes and learning from them. This is how people grow and develop. It might seem strange, but those who have been the most successful in life are those who have made the most mistakes and learned from them.

> *"The only failure in life is the failure to participate."*
>
> Author Unknown

Are you prepared to get it "close enough," and do a conscientious job without doing it perfectly? Have you ever noticed that what you think is "perfect" may not be what the next person considers "perfect?" Being perfect therefore is a no-win.

EXERCISE 2.2.4 Continued:

4. Do you have negative thoughts or worry?
YES / NO

If Yes, on a Scale of 1 to 10, how often do you have negative thoughts, where 1 = Not at all and 10 = All the time?

What's your score? ....

Sabotaging yourself or feeling inferior can manifest in different ways, but frequently it occurs because you latch on to messages in your head which are **not** conducive to positive living.

Some people even go so far as to describe themselves as "worry-warts." Others know that their self-talk is not positive, and they tend to beat up on themselves and limit themselves.

People often say that they always focus on the negative side of things. They say that they are pessimistic. It keeps them awake at night as they "stew" on things. They always seem to look for the down-side.

> **The loudest voice you'll ever hear is your own.**

Yes, the loudest voice you'll ever hear is your own. If you feel inferior, see if you are hanging on to some negative beliefs which are sure to sabotage you. Dispelling, or changing or doing away with these kinds of beliefs can make a world of difference. It can improve your life significantly.

Is the cup half empty or is the cup half full? How you view the world determines how you act and behave in the world.

Self-Sabotage & Inferiority

EXERCISE 2.2.5 Continued:

5. Do you try to fake it on the outside, but know that inside you feel insecure?

YES / NO

If Yes, on a Scale of 1 to 10, how often do you try to present a confident exterior, but inwardly know that you really feel insecure, where 1 = Not at all and 10 = All the time?

What's your score? ....

We all wear our masks. Some fake that they are okay, but underneath confide that they are not. Some wear their external masks so tightly that they over-compensate by being arrogant, abrupt or aggressive. Some are know-it alls. Underneath it all though, they all know within themselves that they are under-confident. They will never let on publicly, though. They are pretenders.

Being prepared to put down the mask, and risk connecting and interacting genuinely, is a pathway to more effective and satisfying communication. But of course, there is the fear that doing so will mean that you lose your whole identity.

You may want to be different, but there is a fear in letting go, and so many choose to hide behind the gruff exterior, the arrogance, and being the know-it-all which acts as their armor and their protection.

> *"No one can make you feel inferior without your consent."*
>
> Author Unknown

Coping with Inferiority

Many people self-sabotage and feel inferior. They learn to be less than that which they ought to be – less than their potential. In other words, they learn to feel inferior. They feel inadequate and think they don't measure up, are second best, and are not good enough.

> **Feelings of inferiority are learned – therefore, they can be unlearned!**

The good news is that if feelings of inferiority are learned, they can be *"unlearned."* Inferiority is really only a bad habit; ***a bad thinking habit!*** Habits can be changed, but not without effort. So how do you re-learn to be confident, relaxed, and more satisfied?

> Mark came in to see me because he realized that he was limiting his career prospects, his relationships as well as

life generally by his self-sabotage. He was a computer technician who did not feel comfortable around people and generally felt stressed.

He said that it was okay when he worked in the back of the computer shop by himself repairing computers or building PCs, but once he had to go out on the road and visit customers he became very stressed. Further, he said that socially, he was okay meeting people, but did not like to get close to them and did not follow up with further outings or get-togethers. He admitted to feeling fear about getting close to others. His only friends were a couple of "no-hopers" who he knew thought he was alright because he "couldn't fail in their eyes."

Mark talked about his family and his upbringing and in particular, his rather harsh, somewhat vindictive father. He fully recalls being constantly criticized by father and certainly recalled the time that his father yelled at him saying, "You'll never have any friends" and "You'll never amount to anything."

He never felt that he had amounted to much and felt that with others socially for example, they were just filling in time with him chatting and talking and would really like to be talking to someone else much more interesting than him.

Yet part of him wondered if there was something more out there for him. One thing was for sure, he was very unhappy and he was fed up feeling on edge and so stressed especially around others. He wanted to learn how to be more relaxed, how to connect with others more effectively ("I just want to be normal") and how to stop his self-sabotage.

Inferiority Feelings Are a Hallucination

Where did you learn to feel "inferior?" Who told you that you were shy? Who said you weren't good enough? That sports was not your best point? That you're not gifted educationally? That you're not as good as your brother or sister?

Who used to put you down, dominate you, criticize you? – "Don't speak until you're spoken to," "Children should be seen and not heard," "Don't be stupid," "What's the matter with you?" "Haven't you got a brain?" "You're hopeless!" "Why are you always so clumsy?" "Why can't you be as [smart, intelligent, brainy, nice] as [insert name]?" "Why can't you grow up?"

Who used to call you names? Who compared you to others? Who bullied you (physically, emotionally, verbally)? Was someone else in the family the "favorite?" Did you always appear to be "last?" Did you often seem to "miss out?"

Usually, it comes from your mother or father (or both) or your guardians. Occasionally, it comes from a brother or sister – usually older. Parents are well-intentioned in their efforts, but somehow good intentions get misinterpreted or go astray. Maybe your parents gave it their very best shot, but somehow or other, you got it wrong. Maybe despite all their good parenting and their wise counsel, you just mis-perceived it and mis-heard it all.

Perhaps it was a schoolteacher who was critical or picked on you. Maybe it was our antiquated education system, which focuses on what you got wrong instead of what you got right. It's an outdated system that uses a lot of "red ink," and highlights what needs to be corrected instead of emphasizing what you've done well.

Maybe it was our society and its media advertising machine, including newspapers, magazines, television and the internet, which all push and blast us about having the perfect body, the "in" look, the best of the best, and state that unless we have "whiter than white" teeth, wear the very latest in designer-label clothing, or drive the coolest set of wheels, we are not going to make it. We are not up to the mark. We are simply not successful.

The sad part is that when this happens, you actually believe that what you heard from your parents, your teachers and the media is the *truth* – that you're not good enough, that you don't measure up. Perhaps your parents actually did say these kinds of things or perhaps instead, they did do it right, but you simply misperceived. Irrespective, you believed it to be the truth.

As children, we take it all on board as literal. Concrete. Real.

You write it onto the DVDs of your mind. You create files that you store away and archive and then bring out and re-play and re-play and re-play. This is your self-sabotage.

Who says though that parents have a monopoly on the truth? Who says they are correct in every judgment of us? Maybe you misheard it anyway. Who says that that grouchy, sour-looking teacher knew what life was all about (clearly, he or she didn't)? Who says that your older brother or sister really knew it all?

The bottom line is that what you learned can often be more fantasy than fact, more myth than reality. Even if it is reality, and you were not the class brain at school, or you're not gifted at sports, who says that that has to limit your future options?

In short, you have made up a fanciful story about yourself. And the story is rubbish. Utter rubbish.

Admitting that you made up a myth about yourself according to your surroundings and how you perceived things at the time when you were growing up is probably letting yourself off lightly.

Let me say it another way: **You created your own hallucination!** You are hallucinating about yourself in a way that is not (or was not) in touch with reality. Sound harsh? You need to see it for what it is.

Now you need to get rid of your "psychotic" view of yourself! You need to stop hallucinating. You need to change these distortions of who you think that you are.

How Do You Change Your Hallucination?

Your bad habits can be changed. Your imagined fantasies can be altered. Of course, this assumes that you really want to change the way you behave and act.

There are, however, no short-cuts.

> **If you're motivated to change, you can change anything – but you have to be motivated.**

Further, it takes sustained work. Rome wasn't built in a day. If you want to lose weight, for example, it takes time and sustained work. You are not going to lose weight or get fit by just thinking about it, or by just managing to go down to the gym on one occasion. Similarly, if you want to change your attitudes and your self-sabotage, it takes time – but it will happen. It definitely will happen.

The following strategies work. But be assured, you've got to want to change and you've got to stick with it until the change occurs. Haven't you experienced enough pain with sabotaging yourself? Isn't it time for change?

Let me say it again in case you missed it – **you have to really want to change and you have to be prepared to stick with it. And the rewards will be there.**

So what are the strategies for change? How do we stop our self-sabotage? How do we become the person that we were really designed to be? How do we start to realize our potential?

That's what we will start to unravel in the next chapter.

Chapter 2 Summary

An inferiority complex, limiting beliefs, and self-sabotage mean the same thing – we lack confidence, feel anxious or embarrassed around others, let ourselves down, or unsuccessfully cover up these inadequacies by being too brash, arrogant or unfeeling.

The first step in addressing the problem is to practice being aware of it. Self-sabotage is learned; we are not born with it. We learn to compare ourselves with others, are frustrated when we don't measure up, and let negative thoughts take over, or wear a mask to try to hide our insecurity.

Growing up, we took the comments of parents, teachers, family, and the media for example, as literal and real, and therefore created our own hallucinations about ourselves being inferior or not good enough. The good news is that these distortions can be unlearned. We just have to want to change for the better.

CHAPTER 3

UNDERSTANDING THE BASICS

Creatures of Habit

In order to change, you may need a **paradigm shift in your thinking.** You may need to introduce yourself to **new ways of thinking.** You may need to shift out of your comfort zone – **move out of the comfort zone and into what can be called the courage zone!**

I know it's a paradox, but the more you live life in the courage zone, the more you experience the spice of life. This is where you are challenged, stimulated, and experience variety, and where life gives you the best it has to offer. It gives you a quality life. Sounds strange, doesn't it? But it's true. Living on the "edge," as they say, is scary for all of us, but it's also the most rewarding way of living.

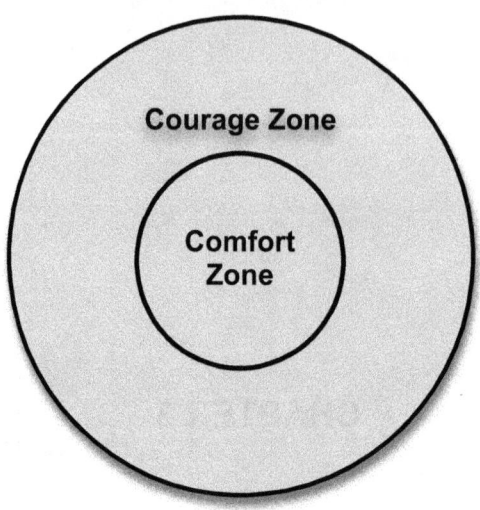

Most people don't like moving out of their comfort zone, and that's why they don't achieve or succeed. Then they often blame their circumstances for their lack of success, or blame others, or make excuses, or say that they're down on their luck or the timing just wasn't right.

"Deeply ingrained assumptions or generalizations or even pictures influence how we understand the world and how we take action."

Senge

You may need to challenge your ingrained assumptions or generalizations about how you understand your world and how, therefore, you behave or take action. These ingrained ways that we have of seeing our world are like wearing a pair of sunglasses. Our whole view of the world gets tainted. Then we behave and act in ways that are consistent with our world-view.

For example, if you see yourself as being born on the "wrong side of the tracks," or as not having attended the best school, then you might behave and act in ways that are consistent with this perspective. You might put yourself down, not venture out, down-play your successes (or really play them up excessively!), avoid particular places or people, and so on.

In essence, we actually create pictures and meanings to understand our lives. These pictures or DVDs that we create are emotionally laden and charged, and direct our actions and responses. Some of those pictures and meanings may have to change!

"We don't see things as they are, we see things as we are."

Anais Nin

When the student is ready, the teacher appears.

Let's find a way to change your paradigms, your assumptions, and your pictures. Let's first look at how you think and how to change thinking patterns.

Thinking

Thinking....ever thought about thinking? We think about our lives by asking questions. Do you know how many questions it has been suggested go through our minds every day both at a conscious and sub-conscious level? It has been estimated that the average person asks **60,000 questions per day!** Right now you're probably asking yourself whether this is true or not!

Admittedly, it's not possible to verify that you actually ask 60,000 questions per day, but even if it's half that number, that's a lot of questions that go through our heads daily. We have busy heads! Busy heads indeed.

Moment by moment we are thinking, and moment by moment we are asking questions in our head.

> **Thinking is nothing more than a series of asking and answering questions.**

In a coaching course that I participated in a while back in California, it was suggested to us that, generally speaking, "WE DON'T LIKE TO THINK." I was taken aback by this as was the rest of the class. "What do you mean that we don't like to think?" I said to myself.

The suggestion put to us by the faculty of that course was that if we really did like to think, we wouldn't go back over **90 - 95% of the same thoughts and stuff all of the time.** We keep returning to the same old kinds of thoughts. Only about 5 – 10% of our thinking is new or original thinking.

> *"The mind once stretched to extended dimensions, never returns to its original dimensions."*
>
> *Author unknown*

This book provides a chance to create some new thoughts and new ways of thinking, and new ways of gaining perspective on yourself. (You may already have gained some new insights and perspectives to this point. There's much more to come.)

So, it's about increasing that 5 - 10% of new or original thought into, say, 15% or even 20%.

> *"The significant problems that we face cannot be solved by the same level of thinking that created them."*
>
> Albert Einstein

Living Up to Your Potential

Now, ask yourself 2 key questions. Take a moment or two to really think about these questions. First, **how much are you living up to your potential?**

Give a percentage score on your actual performance rating; 0% - 100%. Fill out the box below.

> **% Score =**

Now, w**hat stops you from attaining your potential?** In other words, what gets in the way? What blocks you? What are the barriers? What stops you? Write it down.

....
....
....
....
....
....
....

Those who have taken my workshops have come up with various answers to that question about what stops them, such as...

- Lack of confidence
- Lack of self-belief
- Lack of courage
- Lack of time
- Lack of self-esteem
- Fear of success
- Fear of making a mistake
- Fear of failure

The Primary Emotion

Call it what you will. The real stopper or barrier for most of us is...

F E A R

Whether it's labeled lack of confidence, lack of courage, or something else, at the core it's *fear* that stops us from achieving our potential. You've heard the mnemonic for **FEAR** haven't you?

False
Evidence
Appearing
Real

Think about it. It's true, isn't it? Our fears are usually based on some made-up stuff that we have concocted in our heads, which we start to believe or think is real (e.g., "Oh, I couldn't do that, what if I messed up?" "Oh no, I'm not the [leader, out-going, organized...etc] type, why don't you ask someone else?"). It's not real, but we con ourselves into thinking that it is real, and we feel fear or anxiety as a result.

Behind our fears though is a primary fear that lurks.

Originally, you were loved unconditionally as a baby. People would "goo and gah" at you no matter what you did. You could burp, throw up, and so on, and somehow it was all OK (even cute!).

Somewhere along the line though, things changed, and the love seemed to become more conditional. People were no longer particularly happy when you burped or vomited. They didn't always goo and gah, and they put demands on you, had expectations of you, or even reprimanded you.

So, you had to figure out an alternative strategy. What did you have to do to get the love back? What did you have to do to get others to like you? Well...pleasing others was a good start....as was being perfect. These were two strategies worth trying for instance.

Underneath it all though, because the love seemed more conditional, you formed the basic belief that you were **"not good enough,"** and that as a consequence, you had a further underlying and even more basic belief that because you weren't good enough...**you were not lovable.**

This "fear" means that we cause ourselves to self-sabotage. We stop ourselves.

We stop ourselves from....
...achieving our goals
...realizing our potential
...achieving our mission
...realizing our purpose

We need to break out of this self-sabotage. We need to stop limiting ourselves. We need to stop the self-sabotage and we need to increase the self-confidence.

As I've said, there are 3 major strategies. We will go through each in turn. The first one is discussed in the next chapter.

Adrian was, for all intents and purposes, a successful advertising and marketing man. He came into my office on the advice of a trusted friend who told Adrian that he needed to get some coaching to help him.

Adrian sat down and said that he needed help. He said that he was 55 years old and he'd never quite made it. He hadn't achieved what he'd wanted in life, and now, at 55, the issue had become paramount for him. He was running out of time. He hadn't become wealthy in the way that he'd wished. He hadn't done it for himself and more importantly, he hadn't done it for his family. He was now desperate.

He wanted some "blue chip" clients who were big corporate types and who paid well. As we talked, he got into his basic beliefs. When pushed, he confided that as a young boy, his mother had always said, "Don't blow your own trumpet," and "Don't stand out."

I asked him if he was not prepared to tell others what he'd done and tell others of his successes, then how would they find out? How would others know? How would he attract the kind of clients that he really wanted?

He told me that his mother was now dead. She'd died some years before. However, he still kept her "scripting" or her programming in his head. This programming was the cause of his sabotage. He was sabotaging his potential success. He was sabotaging his wealth creation.

"If you want to be something different, you have to do something different."

Author unknown

Chapter 3 Summary

We are creatures of habit and we tend to live in our comfort zone, but the real juice of life is breaking out of this into the courage zone. It takes courage to learn to be different.

One of the main ways that we are caught in our self-sabotage is through our poor thinking habits. These need to change. In order to fight self-sabotage, we need to adopt new ways of thinking and challenge ourselves to change. We need to identify what stops us from thinking about ourselves more positively.

However, the one thing that always seems to stop us from stepping out and from growing is fear. Similarly, the one thing that keeps us bound up in ourselves is fear. Generally, it is simply the fear that somehow, we are not good enough and worse still, that perhaps we are not lovable. Breaking out of this paradigm is what we are now about.

CHAPTER 4

THE SILENT OPERATOR: YOUR SELF-TALK

Self-talk? "What is self-talk?" you might well ask. Your self-talk is sometimes referred to as self-chatter, silent self-talk, or internal dialogue.

Self-talk is the internal voices you hear anywhere you happen to be – in cafes, in restaurants, in the shopping mall, in the office, in the factory, in the car, at home. You hear them at work and play. You hear them in meetings or in crowds or while you're alone.

It is the thoughts that run through your head as you read this now. Hear them? More than this though, it is the myriad of thoughts that constantly flow through your mind every second, every minute and every waking moment of your day.

Your self-talk represents your beliefs. How you weigh things up. How you assess things. What you think about things. Your opinions.

No doubt you have seen some demented person in the street talking out loud to themselves and having conversations with themselves. Well, that's not much different from what we all do, except we don't do it aloud. We compare, speculate, evaluate, comment, approve, disapprove and judge. It just goes on.

"Success doesn't come from the way you think it does; it comes from the way you think."

Dr. Robert Schuller

You continually have little conversations in your head about all sorts of things. In fact, the mind never seems to switch off. We mistakenly believe that there is this endless tirade and tyranny of thoughts that just naturally happens and rolls us along and that we have no control over this continual flow of thoughts. We delude ourselves, because nothing is farther from the truth – we actually do have control over it.

I've had some clients though, who deny that they have any self-talk. They believe that they don't talk to themselves at all, that they don't think anything to themselves. They say to me, "No Darryl, I don't have any self-talk. I don't talk to myself. Not me." Sadly, I inform them that if that's true...then...they are dead!

You talk to yourself about all kinds of things; about how you performed, about what you said and what you did, what you think of this and what you think of that, what you feel and how you measured up. You talk to yourself about future situations ("What if....") and about past events ("If only...."). You talk to yourself all the time. It never stops.

"As you think, so shall you be."

Dr. Wayne Dyer

Typically, you try to anticipate future events and you rehearse in your head what you will do, how you will say things, how you will dress, and how you will present yourself. Often, in relation to past events, you chastise yourself and are hard on yourself for the things you have done or said (or should have done or said).

Ever thought about the power of those thoughts? Someone once wrote some very wise and profound words...

> ***Watch your thoughts, they become words.***
> ***Watch your words, they become actions.***
> ***Watch your actions, they become habits.***
> ***Watch your habits, they become character.***
> ***Watch your character, it becomes your destiny.***

Thoughts become your destiny! That's right, your destiny. If that's true, you'd better get your thoughts right. You'd better get control of those thoughts.

The secret for those people who seem to get ahead, take risks, are successful and self-confident in life, is that they tend to closely watch their self-talk. It has been estimated that we talk to ourselves at a rate of about 1000-2000 words per minute. Is it any wonder that we go from a mole-hill to a mountain in a split second?

> *"Worry gives a small thing a big shadow."*
>
> — Swedish Proverb

Negative Thoughts

It has also been suggested that most of this silent conversation is one-sided and negative in orientation. Some of my clients have referred to themselves as "worry warts" or pessimists. Others just say that they always "look on the negative side of things" or perhaps expect the worst. Some even say that they always think of the down side so that then they won't get disappointed when things don't work out!

> *"If you keep on saying that things are going to be bad, you have a good chance of being a prophet."*
>
> Isaac Bashevis

C. S. Lewis, in his book *Surprised by Joy*, is even more descriptive and vivid or graphic about self-talk. He says that when he looked inside himself he found "...a zoo of lusts, a bedlam of ambitions, a nursery of fears, a harem of fondled hatreds."

Clinically, as I talk to people intimately about their life and its circumstances, it is clear that many individuals are locked into negative self-talk. It has become a habit.

> *"Two people have been living in you all of your life...One is the ego, garrulous, demanding, hysterical, calculating... The other is the hidden spiritual being, whose still voice of wisdom you have only rarely heard or attended to."*
>
> Sogjal Rinoche
> *The Tibetan Book of Living and Dying*

People seem to **automatically** slip into self-criticism, self-judgment, looking on the worst side of things and expecting the worst. Sometimes these thoughts have been called "gremlins," but they are always negative.

There is a very real sense in which an inferiority complex or self-sabotage is really negative self-talk which has been habit-forming over years. The pessimist, for example, has nothing but negative self-talk going on in their mind. As a person called James Allen once wrote, "A man is literally what he thinks."

> "If you think you can, or think you can't, you're right."
>
> Henry Ford

> I remember a woman who came to see me feeling quite depressed and teary about an arm injury and saying things like, "Why me?" and "Will it ever get better?" We discussed her self-talk.
>
> Interestingly, she later recited to me how during the following week she had been feeling very low and went into a major shopping center in the city of Adelaide.
>
> At the entrance to the shops, she encountered a blind boy making his way along with a white stick. Immediately, this prompted her to snap out of her negative thinking and self-pity and instead, she said things like, "At least I can see and I have all my faculties," "I'm not so bad off," "I have a lot to be thankful for."
>
> She felt much more positive all day and through the following week.

> As an aside, because she also felt much more positive and acted accordingly, she noticed that her work colleagues responded more cheerfully towards her too!

What Triggers Negative Self-Talk?

Where does the self-talk come from? How does it happen?

In your environment, you are surrounded by "triggers" – situations or a series of events which affect your mood, your feelings or your emotions. Moment by moment, there are things happening around us that we are reacting to – our triggers. Sometimes too, these triggers are internal in that we just start to think about things or "stuff."

In between the trigger, or what is happening in your external environment or surrounds, and your emotions or how you feel about the situation is your thoughts.

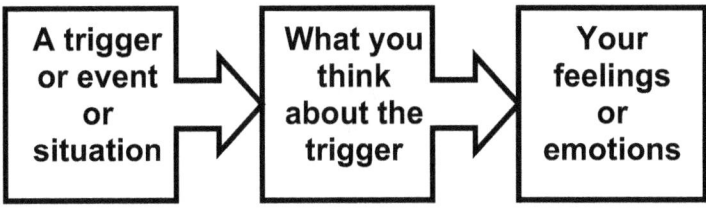

The meanings that you give to things determines how you feel. Your thoughts determine your mood or feelings. Think happy thoughts, feel happy. Think sad thoughts, feel sad. It's straightforward, really.

How do you fix your self-talk? How do you feel better? The answers may not be what you want to hear. It may not be the good news story that you want.

No easy tricks here – no silver bullets – no short-cuts. Life isn't like that – the things that are worth the most usually require the most effort or sacrifice. **Good things take time.**

> **Our thoughts move us from a mole-hill to a mountain in a split second.**

Remember, you can move from a mole-hill to a mountain in a split second! Your thoughts are ballistic. They move at rocket speed. Sometimes, you think so quickly and fast that you can make yourself dizzy.

> *"You can complain because roses have thorns, or you can rejoice because thorns have roses."*
>
> Zig Ziglar

The Silent Operator: Your Self-Talk

> Are you an optimistic person?
>
> A positive person?
>
> There are always two sides to a coin.
>
> Which side do you *choose* to look at?
>
> The positive or the negative?
>
> *You get to choose.*

**There are two sides to every coin!
Every time.**

How Does Negative Self-Talk Work?

It is called the **A-B-C-D** of thinking. It is simple really. It goes like this – see the flow chart below and Figure 4.1.

THE A-B-C-D OF THINKING

A TRIGGER / EVENT / SITUATION
Something triggers or sets you off.

1. It could be an <u>external</u> trigger like a phone call, what someone says or does or something that you see or hear.

2. It could be an <u>internal</u> trigger like a daydream or stream of thoughts.

3. Sometimes it can be both external <u>and</u> internal.

YOUR THOUGHTS
You weigh up the trigger or the event, which is given meaning by you such that you have a series of thoughts that go round in your head, and this is typically called your self-talk – it cuts in automatically and is often negative!

YOUR FEELINGS
You feel emotion. Your feelings are created by your thoughts.
(You think sad thoughts, you feel sad, etc.)

The Silent Operator: Your Self-Talk

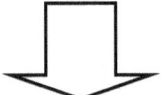

YOUR ACTIONS or REACTION
You react. Your action, reaction, response or behavior is a result of your feelings.

In a nutshell, all your experiences are assessed or processed by you and given some meaning via your thoughts or self-talk, which then determines how you feel.

To change your feelings therefore;

- you need to change either your **situation** (e.g., leave your job, sell your house, change your relationship, do something different)

OR

- change your **thoughts or self-talk** about the situation or trigger (e.g., "I'm fortunate to have a job and this really is no big deal in the whole scheme of things," "I recognise that he / she has done a lot for me and they really have some positive points that I shouldn't overlook.")

OR

- change **BOTH your situation and your thoughts**

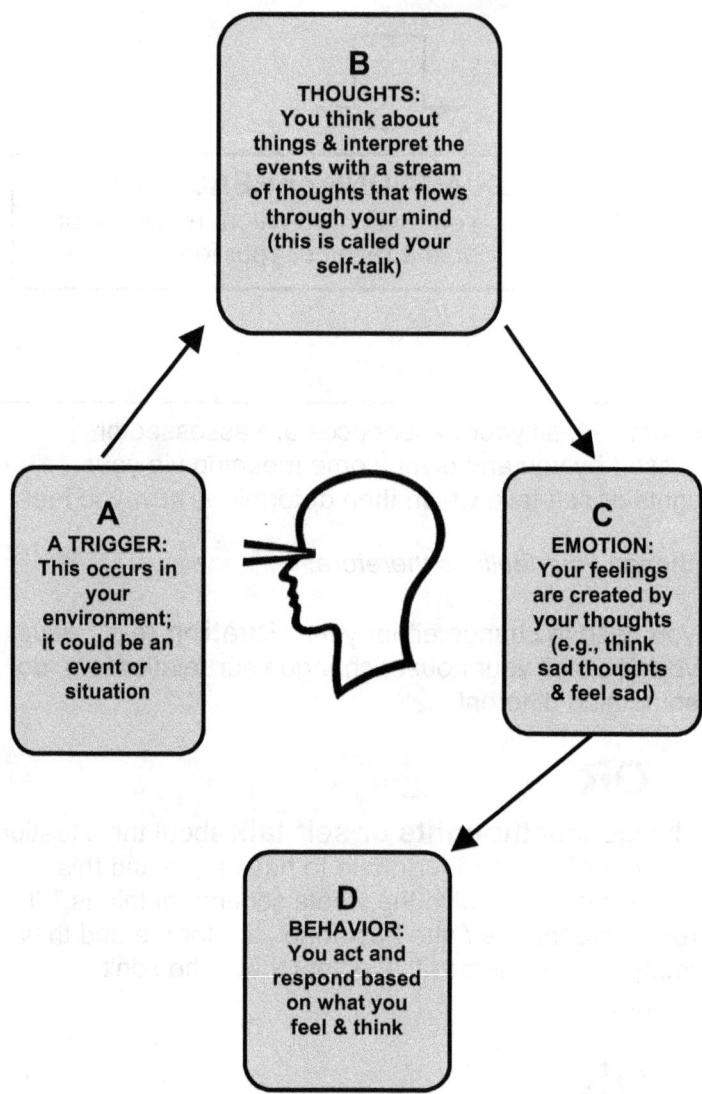

Figure 4.1
All experiences are processed through your brain and given conscious meaning before you experience an emotional response and then behave accordingly.

Changing your thoughts though, is not easy. You may have been thinking negatively for a long time. As I've said before, it would have become a habit by now. So, how do you do it, especially if there is no silver bullet and no quick fix?

The old adage "Count your blessings," is a wise saying. Better still, as well as counting your fortunes, try thinking positively and your life will start to be transformed (more about this in the next chapter).

First though, let's look at a very practical beginning step.

A very effective way to start your day is, when you wake up, to immediately count your blessings. It has the effect of gearing your brain into a positive mode rather than the alternative. Instead of moaning about having to get out of bed or being tired or not wanting to go to work, try a different method. It really works. For example, try this exercise.

EXERCISE 4.1:

Write down all the things that you can be thankful for each morning when you wake up. Make a list of 10 things. For example, "I'm thankful that I have a solid roof over my head," "I'm thankful that I'm alive and healthy," "I'm thankful that I can work and be productive," "I'm thankful for my children," "I'm thankful that I can see," and so on.

My Thankful List:

1.
....

2.
....

3.
....

4.
....

5.
....

6.
....

7.
....

8.
....

9.
....

10.
....

Now, as soon as you wake up, go through this list and say them in your head, or out loud if you wish.

Try this for 10 days – every morning – and see if it makes any difference to you.

Are you up for this? Then do it. What have you got to lose?

Make up your list and put it by your bedside or close at hand. Have this book next to your bed or perhaps transfer your list onto another piece of paper.

*"We can do only what we think we can do.
We can be only what we think we can be.
We can have only what we think we can have.
What we do, what we are, what we have, all depend upon what we think."*

Robert Collier

Chapter 4 Summary

We are constantly self-talking or chatting internally to ourselves. It never stops. The power though of these inner thoughts is profound in that ultimately, they can determine our destiny. They are so powerful that we are usually not even aware that they are wielding a negative force over our lives.

Our self-talk has to change for us to change our insecurities. For this to occur, we need to know the formula for how our thoughts happen. The A-B-C-D formula shows the way that we are triggered by events which we think about which then means that we experience emotion which then determines how we act and behave.

We need to break the habit of negative thinking and silent self-criticism by recognizing the situations that trigger them as well as the fact that we can alter and control our thinking patterns. As a first step, the Thankful exercise is used to help start thinking positively.

"What's one of the major differences between those who are successful and those who are not? The way they think."

Darryl Cross

CHAPTER 5

THE PROCESS FOR POSITIVE SELF-TALK

What's the Process for Eliminating Negative Self-Talk?

How do you know that you have actually just sabotaged yourself? How do you know if you have limiting beliefs? What could you use that would indicate that you have just slipped up in your thinking?

Answer: you feel bad. Yes, you know it by your feelings. Your feelings give you the clue that all is not well with you. When you feel bad, you have usually self-sabotaged, let yourself down or somehow not met expectations.

EXERCISE 5.1:

How do you really FEEL when you feel "bad?" How do you feel bad? In what way? How would you personally describe it?

Write it down.

....

....

....

....

There is a step process for being able to reduce your self-talk and get your negative thoughts under control. The process works. However, **the key to the process is listening to your "emotional guidance system."** This is your emotional barometer. It is critical that you listen to your barometer because it is there to guide you. You need to "read" it. Get in touch with it. Know how you're feeling at any point in time. Take time to listen to your emotions. This may be strange for some of you, but let me reassure you, that your emotional guidance system is your very best friend. It's your ally; it does guide you.

In other words, you need to be sufficiently aware and sufficiently in touch with yourself to know when you're feeling badly. If you're not aware when you're "out of

The Process For Positive Self-Talk

sorts" as the saying goes, or not aware when you're feeling badly, then you have little chance (if any) of being in a position of intervening with your negative thoughts. Your emotions should tell you if you've messed up.

In short, if you're feeling badly, it's probably because your thinking just fouled up or you're thinking faulty thoughts.

Basically though, in my experience, there are only **5 major negative emotions,** i.e. ways that you feel "bad." I don't want to make life sound too simplistic, but essentially, you only have to look out for the "**big 5**." You might have various names for these emotions, but there are still only really five. Look at the list below.

1. **Anxiety**
   (we say that we're stressed, uptight, nervous, anxious, scared, fearful)

2. **Depression**
   (we say that we're flat, down, feeling blue, feeling "off")

3. **Anger**
   (we say that we're annoyed, PO'ed, ticked off, irritated, "mad as hell")

4. **Guilt**
   (we say that we're embarrassed, ashamed, or feeling guilty)

5. **Resentment**
   (we say that we're resentful or feeling bitter)

So, the process for turning around negative thoughts begins with recognizing that you're feeling badly. You don't feel good. This is your emotional guidance system.

So, check out this **5-step process**, and then I'll tell you how to implement the process.

STEP 1: Are you feeling bad?
(See "C" on Page 52)

Whenever you feel bad, see if you can identify or label the feeling (e.g., anxious, depressed, angry, etc.) and maybe rate its intensity on a 1 to 10 scale where 1 = None and 10 = maximum emotion (e.g., anxiety [5], depression [8]).

STEP 2: What started it? What was the trigger? (See "A" on Page 52)

Identify the triggering event or situation, which can be an external event (e.g., a phone call, a meeting, what someone said), or an internal event (e.g., a daydream, stream of thoughts), or both.

STEP 3: What went through your head? What negative questions did you ask yourself? What negative statements did you say to yourself? What was

your self-talk? What must you be believing for you to feel this way? (See "B" on Page 52)

Write down the exact automatic, irrational, negative thoughts, i.e. *"What must I be saying to myself about this triggering event or situation to make me feel so bad?"* The answers are the irrational, negative thoughts.

STEP 4: Counteract, turn around, reverse, dispute and challenge those initial negative thoughts.

Make the thoughts positive, or dispute how true your original faulty thoughts were, i.e. do a "Re-Think." How can you get another perspective on it? How can you flip your thoughts around? For example:

1. <u>Are you saying "always" or "never?"</u> Are you drawing conclusions on the basis of only one incident and giving yourself a hard time by saying "always" or "never," or are you exaggerating by using the words "always" and "never?" Question any over-generalizations you are making.

2. <u>Are you jumping to conclusions</u>? Question the evidence. ("Where's the evidence that...?") Maybe

you've drawn a conclusion without any real evidence to support it.

3. <u>Are you seeing things as either black or white</u>? Question any simplistic black-or-white thinking – seeing things as being only one extreme or the other, or as only good or only bad. In the real world, there are many shades of grey.

4. <u>Are you imagining the worst</u>? Question whether you are seeing things as the being "the end of the world," "catastrophic," "terrible," "horrible," or "awful," and instead, replace these with words like "unpleasant" or "unfortunate" or "inconvenient."

5. <u>Are you blowing things out of proportion</u>? Instead of focusing on what's wrong and blowing it out of all proportion, look at any positive aspects that might have occurred.

6. <u>Are you taking it all personally</u>? Stop taking things personally and blaming yourself, and instead recognize that you may only be partly responsible or not at all responsible.

STEP 5: Write down the "Re-Think" thoughts.

Write down, replace and counteract the negative, faulty thoughts with positive, constructive, rational thoughts.

To follow this 5-Step Process, use the **Thoughts Record Sheet** that is outlined briefly below – an extensive Thoughts Record Sheet is included as an **appendix** to this book (see pages 132-133). **Also included is a sample of a Thoughts Record Sheet already filled out to give you a better idea of what it means to turns your thoughts around.** This is an important exercise to do. No, this is a critical exercise to do!

THOUGHTS RECORD SHEET

Day, Date & Time	Negative Emotion (Intensity 1-10)	Triggering Event	Irrational, Negative Thoughts	Rational, Positive Thoughts

Feel free to photocopy the Thoughts Record Sheet in your Appendix or make up your own because you will be using this sheet over and over for a number of days and times in order to help you break your poor thinking habits.

How Do You Actually Implement This Process in Daily Practice?

A **practical tip** to help you follow these steps is to carry a piece of paper with you through the day, and whenever you feel badly, quickly scribble down the time, where you were, what triggered it and how you felt. That takes no more than just a few seconds.

When you get home at night, pull out your Thoughts Record Sheet as shown above (you can also draw up your own similar to the one shown in the Appendix) and fill out the first 4 columns from your scribblings during the day.

Then comes the interesting part. Write down your negative thoughts *exactly* as you said it in your head. Verbatim. They'll come back to you as you recall the trigger and the situation.

Then take the time to force yourself to write down alternative positive thoughts – counteract, turn around and revise your original negative thoughts to get another perspective on it all. This shouldn't take more than about 10 minutes. Not a bad investment of time.

Writing it down and going through this process means that your brain picks up on the changes more clearly and sets you up for success the next time, especially if you continue to do your writings for a number of weeks until the ideas become entrenched and you can think more positively without writing it all down. Then it becomes a habit – a new thinking habit. To reiterate:

- **Get a piece of paper and slip it into your pocket, your purse, your wallet, etc.**

- **During the day as events or situations unfold, and you start to feel badly, quickly scribble down the time and place, the trigger and how you felt.**

- **At night, once you're home, take out your Thoughts Record Sheet (see the Appendix), fill it out properly based on your scribbles, and then write down your automatic, negative thoughts that you had at the time.**

- **Then, make yourself re-write these thoughts into positive thoughts in order to gain a new perspective.**

So, why bother with writing it down? Can't I just do this "re-think" and turn it around in my head?

No. Remember, you have created a bad thinking habit over time, probably over years or decades. You know how to have negative, faulty thoughts and they just automatically cut in. It's second nature to think poorly of yourself, to beat up on yourself, to put yourself down and to see things as "half empty." You're good at it! You're well practiced!

You know that you have limiting beliefs about yourself. Don't think that now you can just simply turn these entrenched, crusty old habits around in a blink! Your brain won't catch on unless you actually write it down and see it in black and white. To start you off, attempt the exercise below on this page.

EXERCISE:
Spend time thinking about the last time you felt badly or perhaps the times that you repeatedly feel badly. Then try to work out what triggered it and, more importantly, what you said in your head about it. Now, try turning those thoughts around and reversing them. This will give you a chance to practice flipping around those negative thoughts and writing them down in a more positive way.

Start using your Thoughts Record Sheet today by writing down any times that you can recall that you felt badly. Think back to a time when you felt bad. What started it? What did you think to yourself? Now, how would you force yourself to turn that around? How could you have thought differently? (See the **sample** in the **A**ppendix in this book on page 133.)

You'll be surprised by what you see and discover.

"For as long as I can remember, I've suffered from anxiety and low self-esteem. I know that I'm a negative or pessimistic thinker. My family calls me a worry-wart. My local doctor insisted that he refer me to a psychologist. I really didn't want to go, but decided in the end that I would.

The therapy challenged the way that I saw things and challenged my habitual negative way of thinking, and I became more realistic in my perceptions. I was able, for example, to see things that I would have once seen as negative or awful in a more positive light.

I saw the psychologist for about four months and occasionally go back for a 'refresher.' But I can honestly say that it changed my 'head space' and certainly changed my life around.

Looking back, I think that my constant anxiety made me depressed. And that meant low self-confidence.

I still remember, though, the quote that I learned: 'It's not what happens to you that's important, it's your interpretation of what happens to you that's important.' It's true you know."

Chapter 5 Summary

Feeling bad is the clue that we are self-sabotaging through negative self-talk. Our emotional guidance system should let us know when thoughts are making us feel anxious, depressed, angry, guilty or resentful.

A 5-step process and a Thoughts Record Sheet are introduced to help us use our emotional guidance system and allow us to track our negative thinking.

Importantly, we then need to write down our experiences and turn around our thinking on paper or the lessons will not sink in. The brain needs to see it written down in order for it to catch on that there is a new way of thinking that is more positive.

"When people will not weed their own minds, they are apt to be overrun with nettles."

Horace Walpole

CHAPTER 6

SELF-TALK TRAPS FOR BEGINNERS

Examples of Turning Negative Thoughts into Positive Thoughts

Examples of how you might turn around your automatic negative thoughts into a better perspective include the following:

Your first, automatic, negative thoughts	Your re-think, positive thoughts
"Oh no! What a day this is going to be!"	"This looks like a busy day, but I can only take things one step at a time. At least tonight I can rest and relax and chill out."

"This has ruined my life."	"My life is still here. Sure it was really unfortunate and I really wouldn't wish what I went through on anyone, but I have learned some important lessons. This can make me stronger as a result."
"I can't stand that person."	"I don't have to like him, I just have to have a working relationship with him and besides, why would I allow my peace to be disturbed by letting someone like that get under my skin?"
"I'm completely hopeless with time – I miss deadlines all the time."	"Time is an issue for me and this is an opportunity to learn a lesson here. It's not beyond me – I just have to plan this one through. If I can master this one, I can master almost anything!"
"What if I blow it? That would be terrible."	"Where's the evidence that I'm going to mess it up? That's ridiculous. I've prepared well, and besides, if I get a question I don't know, it's really OK to say that I don't know or that I'll find out the answer."

Self-Talk Traps for Beginners

One of the forefathers of "cognitive re-structuring," or turning your thoughts around, was Dr. Albert Ellis. He observed that there are at least **8 main irrational or faulty thoughts** that are common within the general population. The 8 most common faulty thoughts are:

Common Faulty Thinking	Reverse into Positive Thinking
1. Everyone needs to love or like me.	There are certainly some people in my life who love and like me. I might feel disappointed or lonely when that doesn't happen for everyone, but it's not the end of the world. I can definitely take constructive steps though to make and keep better relationships.
2. I'm only any good if I make no mistakes, am always competent and always achieve.	I want to do some things well, most of the time. Like everybody, I will occasionally fail or make a mistake. Then I might feel badly, but I can cope with that, and I can learn from the mistakes in order to do better next time.

3. It is dreadful, catastrophic, nearly the end of the world, when things aren't how I want them to be, or don't go the way I want them to.	Things don't always go the way that I want. Is that really so bad? It might be disappointing when things aren't how I expect, but I can cope with that. Usually I can take positive steps to make things more as I would like them to be, but if I can't, it doesn't help me to exaggerate my disappointment.
4. Things happen to me outside my control, so I can't do anything about it and that makes me feel bad.	My problems may be influenced by factors outside my control, but my thoughts and actions also influence my problems, and they **are** under my control. It's not what happens to me that's important, it's what I do about it that's important.
5. If something might be unpleasant, concerning or frightening, I should worry a lot about it.	Worrying about something that might go wrong won't stop it from happening, it only makes me unhappy now! Besides, 9 out of 10 things that you worry about never happen. I can certainly take steps to prepare for any possible problems, and that's as much as anyone can do. There's no point in dwelling on the future or the past.

6. It is easier to put off something difficult or unpleasant than it is to face up to it.	Putting off problems doesn't make them go away or make them any easier, it just gives me longer to worry about them. Facing difficult situations might make me feel bad at the time, but I can cope with that. Besides, it is easier to get it over and done with.
7. I need to depend on someone stronger than myself.	It's good to get support from others when I want it, but the only person I really need to rely on is myself.
8. My problems were caused by some events in my past, so that's why I have my problems now.	My problems may have started in some past events, but blaming my past is not going to help me fix the issues or move forward. My present thoughts and actions, however, **are** under my present control.

Key Words and Phrases to Watch Out For

Whenever you find yourself feeling "bad," it may well be that you have sabotaged yourself or limited yourself by using one of the following "trip-ups."

Watch out for these **common words and phrases** that we often use. You might consider that they are insignificant, but don't be fooled – **they are powerful enemies of positive thinking**! As I've said before, words do matter. The kind of language that you use sends powerful messages to your brain. Watch the way that you talk.

Types of Thinking	Examples & Descriptor Words & Phrases
Blowing it out of Proportion: Taking the negative details and amplifying them, while at the same time filtering out any positive aspects of a situation. Looking at the threats in a situation instead of looking at the challenges and opportunities.	"I've lost my job – I'm ruined – it's the end." "I've had an argument with my spouse – I should never be married."
Black & White Thinking: Things are black or white, good or bad. You have to be perfect, or you're a failure. There is no middle ground. There are no shades of grey.	"Coming in 2nd is not good enough." "There are no prizes for finishing 2nd." "Why didn't you get an 'A' grade instead of a 'B' grade?"
Over-generalization: Coming to a general conclusion based on a single incident or piece of evidence.	Saying words like "nobody," "everybody," "always" and "never." "Nobody likes me." "You always do that." "I never get a turn." "This always happens to me." "I always lose out."

Self-Talk Traps for Beginners

Mind Reading: Without their saying so, you know what people are feeling and why they act the way they do. In particular, you are able to divine how people are feeling toward you.	"I know what you're feeling." "What you believe is...." "I know what you think of me."
Catastrophizing: Expecting disaster. You notice or hear about a problem and make mountains out of molehills. Stress is exaggerated. Problems are exaggerated.	Saying words like "terrible," "awful," "horrible," and phrases like, "I can't stand it," "It's the end of the world."
Comparing with Others: Comparing yourself to others, trying to determine who is smarter, better looking, better dressed, richer, etc.	"She's better than me." "He's got all the looks and talent." "I wish I was fun like she is." "I wish I was slim like her."
Personalizing: Thinking that everything people do or say is some kind of reaction to you.	"Why are they looking at me all the time?" "What's wrong with me?" "I must look weird."
External Control Myth: If you feel externally controlled, you see yourself as helpless, a victim of fate. You have no power. You have no choices. You are impotent.	"I can't." "It's too overwhelming." Instead say, "I won't," or "How can I...?"
Internal Control Myth: The fallacy of internal control has you responsible for the pain and happiness of everyone around you.	"It's all my fault." "I did this to them."

Fantasy of Fairness: You feel resentful because life's not fair. You think you know what's fair, but other people won't agree with you.	"It's not fair." "It's never fair." "Life's not fair."
Blaming Others: Holding other people responsible for your pain or your situation when things have not gone as you would have wished.	"They made me do it." "It's my teachers' fault." "They made me fail." "The department is messed up." "Management is hopeless." "My boss is hopeless."
Shoulds: You have a list of ironclad rules about how you and other people should act. People who break the rules anger you and you feel guilty if you violate the rules. You set unrealistic standards of perfection for yourself.	Every time you use a "should," you "sh_t" on yourself – e.g., saying words like, "should," "must," "ought," and "have to" only serve to act as failure statements.
Fantasy of Change: You expect that other people will change to suit you if you just pressure or cajole them enough. You need to change other people.	"Once he's married to me, I'll change him." "Why can't she be different?"
Reinforcing Failure: Rather than condoning yourself for your failure, instead look for any lessons learned and focus on the behavior rather than your weaknesses.	"I'm hopeless." "I'm so dumb." "I'm an idiot." "That's just like me," instead of, "Next time, I'll…"

Self-Talk Traps for Beginners

Being Right: You are continually on trial to prove that your opinions and actions are correct. Being wrong is unthinkable and you will go to any length to demonstrate your rightness.	"This is what I think (and what you think doesn't matter)." "I know I'm right (and what you think doesn't count)." "This is the way it is (there is no other)."
Heaven's Reward Fallacy: You expect all of your sacrifices and self-denial to pay off, as if there were someone keeping score. You feel bitter when the reward doesn't come and when others don't "pay up."	"After all I've done." "They're so ungrateful." "I did this for them, but they…"
Putting Yourself Down: Personally blaming yourself for your failures, mistakes or problems, and reinforcing your failures.	Saying "I am," instead of "I do," e.g., "I am a failure, I am hopeless," instead of, "I did not pass my test," "I did not study hard enough."
Jumping to Conclusions: You generalize from one or two incidents or characteristics into negative global judgment.	"They're sure to think I'm a fool."
Living Negatively in the Past: Going back over "spilt milk" or re-analyzing the past in hind-sight is of little value – what's done is done – it's over.	"If only…" "I wish…"

Living Negatively in the Future: Trying to anticipate events and surmise what might happen. This is wasted energy.	"What if…"

Chapter 6 Summary

Specific examples are provided to show how to re-think our thoughts positively and how to get things into perspective.

The 8 most common irrational or faulty thoughts are also listed as well as ways in which we can turn them around and make them more positive.

The key words and phrases that we use which are certain to lead us into negative thinking are identified. We need to watch out for these "trip-ups" in that they can easily lead us into a downward spiral.

CHAPTER 7

SELF-TALK QUESTIONS & ANSWERS

As we said at the beginning of this book, thinking is the process of both asking and answering questions.

Negative Questions

So, if you ask yourself **negative or dumb questions** ...what will you get?

...negative answers!

What you need to understand is that your brain is really your best friend and it tries to help you out with the questions that you ask. So, for example, if you make a mistake and you immediately ask yourself, "Why am I such an idiot?" your brain will try to find you an appropriate answer and search for an appropriate answer such as, "Because you always muck up that's why" or "You're just like your father – a no-hoper" and so on. What's the point of asking dumb questions to have your brain come up with dumb answers?

Therefore, you need to ask yourself **different** questions (not negative or dumb questions). Instead of the following, how would you ask a different kind of question?

- What if I fail?
- What if I make a mistake or miss something?
- What are they thinking of me?
- Am I doing the right thing?
- How can I show them?
- Why haven't I made it?
- What's wrong with me?
- Why does this always happen to me?
- Why do I always try to make people feel good?
- Am I good enough?
- How come I'm not successful?
- Have I made it?
- Why did I mess up?

How do you ask yourself different kinds of questions?

EXERCISE 7.1:

Take one of those negative questions listed above and re-work it into a positive question.

For example: "Why did I mess up?" could be re-worked into, "What do I need to learn for the next time?" OR "What could I have done better?" So, take another of those questions above and re-work it. Then, for practice, take another one and turn it around.

....
....
....
....
....
....

Negative Statements

Be aware, too, of the statements you say to yourself.

As well as asking ourselves dumb questions like those above (and giving ourselves dumb or negative answers), we also need to make sure that we are giving ourselves **positive statements** and saying positive things to ourselves.

Give yourself positive statements. How would you re-work the following negative statements that we often say to ourselves?

- I really must be thick.
- Gosh, I'm stupid.
- I really messed that up.
- I really made a fool of myself.
- I really am incompetent.
- I really am pretty hopeless at times.
- Others seem to be so much better than I am.
- I wish I could be as good as…
- I'll never be good at this.
- Everyone else seems to be doing so well.

For example;

- "Everyone else seems to be doing so well," could be re-worked into, "Who says everyone else is doing so well?" OR "Where's the evidence that everyone else is doing so well?" OR "Who says that I can't be successful?"

- "I'll never be good at this," could be re-worked into, "I may not be excellent at this right now, but with practice I can certainly improve significantly."

- "I really messed that up," could be turned into "At least I gave it a try and although it certainly didn't go the way I'd hoped, I learnt a lot in the process and I now know how to do it differently next time."

- "I really am pretty hopeless at times," could be re-stated as, "I know I sometimes make mistakes, but we all do, and that's life, so what can I learn from this one?"

Self-Talk Questions & Answers   85

EXERCISE 7.2:

Take another one of those negative statements listed on the previous page and re-work it into a positive statement. Then take another one and turn it around.

....

....

....

....

....

"It isn't what happens to us that affects our behavior, it's our interpretation of what happens to us that affects our behavior."

Dr. Stephen Covey

Chapter 7 Summary

Specific examples are given and exercises introduced regarding rephrasing both negative questions and statements into challenges for positive living.

Ask a dumb question and you'll get a dumb answer. So, be clever enough to learn to ask more appropriate questions of yourself so that you're not prompting your brain to unnecessarily beat up on you.

Further, say positive statements to yourself about who you are and what you have done and get them into perspective rather than just taking the negative view of what you have done.

CHAPTER 8

THE BOLD OPERATOR: YOUR SPOKEN WORD

As well as our silent self-talk, we also talk out loud to ourselves at times. (You may well have heard others talking out loud to themselves too.) The times when we talk out loud are generally the times when we are annoyed with ourselves. When we get really disgruntled with ourselves or want to beat up on ourselves, then we often talk out loud. We might say things like:

- ⇒ What's the matter with me?
- ⇒ Gosh, am I stupid or what?!
- ⇒ Get with it!
- ⇒ You're an idiot!
- ⇒ Grow up!
- ⇒ I'm losing it!
- ⇒ Alzheimer's is setting in!
- ⇒ I'm having a "senior's" moment!

When we say these things out loud, our whole body gets involved – we hear it, we feel it, and our physiology is involved. In other words, OUR BRAIN GETS IT! And BIG time! Your brain (and the rest of you) gets the message and it hits its target. This is NOT the kind of message, though, that we want our brain to get.

So, if your brain "gets it" with these negative messages, what about turning this around and instead, say some positive things out loud to yourself? When I suggest to my clients that they talk out loud to themselves, they look at me strangely. "Are you serious?" "People will think I'm nuts."

Again I explain that it is a powerful message to our brain when we talk out loud in a negative way, so we need to harness this in a positive sense instead. I also reassure them that this process occurs in private – I'm not expecting them to do it in public!

"What you consistently speak with emotional intensity, you will experience, you will create, you will become. The words that you speak with emotional conviction, become the life you live – this is your heaven or your hell."

Anthony Robbins

The Positive Spoken Word

What about turning this whole physiological-brain thing around to your advantage? Sounds corny? Maybe. But it works! Here's how it goes.

STEP 1: Work out a positive statement that you'd like to use to counteract the negative things you say, out loud, to yourself, or to others.

Instead of berating yourself for not speaking up, or not coping, or making a mistake, or not being confident for example, a more positive statement might be:

> *"I am my own person and I enjoy being firmly assertive and speaking my mind."*

> *"I am all I need to be. I have the courage to see things through, and when push comes to shove, my experience will see me through."*

> *"I am a confident person who copes with whatever comes along."*

> *"God has given me gifts to be myself and to be the best that I can be."*

EXERCISE 8.1:

Now write down your own personal statement (you only need to write down one):

....

....

....

....

....

....

....

....

STEP 2: **Get into a place where you are by yourself for some time** (e.g., in the shower, jogging or out walking, or sitting or driving in the car).

STEP 3: **Say the statement out loud, with intensity and with emphasis and meaning.** Shout it out if you have to. Use your body to say it (e.g., gesture, point, stamp your foot, etc.), but say it with meaning!

STEP 4: Do this for up to 10 minutes a day. Talk out loud in the positive so that your conscious and your subconscious mind picks it up. Now I know that this sounds a bit weird, but I can only say that it does work. You may well be worried though, that others might think that you'd finally "lost it" altogether, but as I said, it does impact you and the brain "gets it."

> I remember the male adolescent whose father brought him in to see me because he was a talented football player, but he had recently lost confidence. However, on the weekend, he was playing in a significant game where the State selectors were going to be present to monitor his form and possibly offer him selection in the State team.
>
> Because of the shortness of time in that the game was in less than a week, it was decided to use the technique just outlined above. I explained to him that it all might sound a bit strange, but I was going to ask him to perform a feat where he was going to talk out-loud to himself. He just smiled. He said it didn't matter how weird it was, he really wanted to play well on Saturday. We then went through the whole process.
>
> He took his piece of paper away with his statement written down and seemed keen to try it out.

> He emailed me on the following Monday to say that he was really proud of the way that he played (and his dad was pleased too) and that it was probably one of his best games.
>
> He said that the selectors were impressed.

Many people continue this routine for their entire lives. Are you prepared to continue this for the rest of your life? The rest of my life, you say? Definitely! You eat every day, you sleep every day. Well, this is just as important. **Every day.**

This is your mental energy and survival. Do it as a 21 day trial. Test it out for yourself. What have you got to lose? If you are not convinced that it is imperative to your positive mental health, then stop the exercise.

Chapter 8 Summary

A step-by-step strategy for speaking out-loud positively, rather than negatively is outlined. Of course, we always need to acknowledge that the words we use impact us (as well as others), so it is important to use positive language.

Consider therefore using a strategy where you specifically speak out loud to yourself as a way of influencing your brain and impacting how you feel and behave. It might sound corny, but there are many who vouch for the technique.

"Words are, of course, the most powerful drug used by mankind."

Rudyard Kipling

CHAPTER 9

THE VISUAL OPERATOR: YOUR SELF-PICTURE

Mental and Physical Creations

How hard is it to do a jigsaw puzzle when you have no idea what you are creating and no picture to guide you?

Typically the picture is on the lid of the box that the jigsaw is packaged in and you need to have the picture next to you when you're working on it. You need to know what it looks like while you're putting it together and what it should look like when you're finished.

In the same way, it's important to actually visualize how you would like to be in a personal sense (e.g., confident, happy, relaxed, successfully coping with change, etc.). How would you personally like to be? What would you like your personal "picture" to look like?

Furthermore, visualize what you would like to achieve (i.e., your goals in life) or where you'd like to go in life (e.g., your career, the house you'd like to own, the painting you'd like to do, the father or mother you'd like to be), and see it in your mind's eye. Picture it. See yourself making changes and doing things slightly differently.

The message is to see the picture in your head, feel the emotion that goes with it, and start to live it and make it happen. So, how does this really work?

In life, there are **two creations**; first there is a mental picture, then there is the physical reality. In essence, no picture, no reality. That's just the way it is!

> Florence Chadwick was the first woman to swim the English Channel in both directions. Now, at age 34, her goal was to become the first woman to swim from Catalina Island to the California coast.
>
> On the 4th of July, 1952, she had been swimming for nearly 16 hours, but when she looked ahead, she saw nothing but a solid wall of fog. The sea was like an ice bath and the fog was so dense she could hardly see her support boats. Sharks cruised toward her lone figure, only to be driven away by rifle shots from her support team. Against the frigid grip of the sea, she struggled on – hour after hour – while millions watched on national television.

> Alongside Florence in one of the boats, her mother and her trainer offered encouragement. They told her it wasn't much further. But all she could see was fog. They urged her not to quit. She never, ever had...until then. With only half a mile to go, she asked to be pulled out.
>
> Still thawing her chilled body several hours later, she told a reporter, "Look, I'm not excusing myself, but if I could have seen land I might have made it." It was not fatigue or even the cold water that defeated her. It was the fog. She was unable to see her goal.
>
> Two months later, she tried again. This time, despite the same dense fog, she swam with her faith intact and her goal clearly pictured in her mind. She knew that somewhere behind that fog was land and this time she made it!
>
> Florence Chadwick became the first woman to swim the Catalina Channel, eclipsing the men's record by two hours!

Visualize and It Happens

If you can't (or won't) see it in your mind's eye, don't be surprised when it doesn't happen.

Your self-pictures are made in the recording room of your mind. This is the movie production and direction area. Technically speaking, it's actually the subconscious area of your mind. This is where all the "movies" of life are created complete with memories, action and emotion.

This is where the script-writers, movie directors, producers, editors and so on, all get together to put together the movie production and film that becomes your life. You cast yourself into a script, cast yourself into a role and bring about your character and outcome. You see it, "film" it, and it becomes a reality.

For example, for about 40 years, the high jump record only showed a gradual increase in height. Then something happened. There was a fundamental change in the technique for high jumping and the bar height went up significantly in a very short period of time (see the diagram below showing the rise in height during the 1960's). Once athletes could conceive of a different way of jumping and knew it was possible, new heights were jumped. **What the mind can conceive, the body can achieve.**

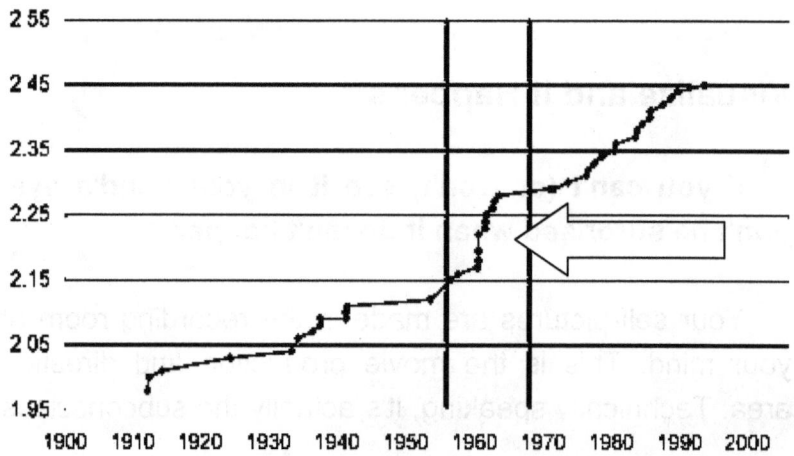

Again on the sports field, there was the 4-minute mile. For years, being able to break the 4-minute mile seemed illusive. One man, however, pursued his dream.

He is Sir Roger Gilbert Bannister (born 1929) who is an English athlete and the first man to run the mile in less than 4 minutes. (Bannister actually became a distinguished neurologist and Master of Pembroke College, Oxford, before retiring in 2001. He is also one of the major shareholders of Birmingham City Football Club.)

The 4-minute mile was once thought to be impossible by informed observers and was considered to be a widely propagated myth cooked up by sportswriters. However, the myth worked. This negative mind set meant that the 4-minute mile was evasive. It was not seen as possible.

Bannister was initially inspired by another runner's remarkable comeback in 1945. However, after the devastation of his failure at the 1952 Olympics, Bannister spent two months deciding whether to give up running. Critically, he decided on a new goal: To be the first man to run a mile in under four minutes.

In other words, he set his goal and he visualized it. Then, he physically intensified his training and did hard intervals. There is a mental creation and then comes the physical creation.

The historic race took place on May 6, 1954, during a meet between British AAA and Oxford University at Iffley Road Track in Oxford. It was watched by about 3,000 spectators. With winds up to 25 miles per hour (40 km/h) prior to the event, Bannister had said twice that he favored not running, and that he would try again at another meet. However, the winds dropped just before the race was scheduled to begin, and Bannister ran. His time was 3 minutes, 59.4 seconds.

Once this time had been broken, just like the high jump record, the 4-minute mile was then broken by a number of other runners and all in quick succession. What the mind can conceive, the body can achieve. In case you missed it, there are always two creations; the mental followed by the physical.

EXERCISE 9.1:

Think of a really embarrassing moment in your life. It might have been when you were younger; maybe it was more recently. Perhaps it was overseas or maybe in your own city or another city. Maybe it was when you were a child, or as an adolescent. It could have been at school, at university, when you were studying, at work, or at play. It could have been in your marriage or to do with relationships.

Jot down a few words to prompt you. Your most embarrassing moment:

....

....

....

....

....

....

Once you've recalled your embarrassing moment, let me ask you a question.

Could you see it in your mind's eye? Could you sense the embarrassment that you felt back then?

Typically, what you did at that time was that you recorded a kind of video or DVD in your mind, and you can recall the emotion that went with it. This is, in a sense, an analogy of what we do in life itself!

Initially, our parents (or care-givers) helped us record some of our more basic DVDs when we were much younger. Unfortunately, when we were young, we sometimes made up "mythical" videos or DVD's about ourselves such as the "I'm not good enough" movie or the "I'll never make it" movie or the "poor me" movie or the "It's not fair" movie and so on. You get the point.

Once recorded however, these videos or DVDs keep on playing in our mind (whether we like it or not) and even when we are adults. We might look grown up on the outside, but we keep playing these "lame" videos on the inside. Talk about self-sabotage!

Sometimes we feel the tension, the stress and the emotion as the DVDs replay. But what is important to know too, is that **they just kick in automatically**. **In short, we have an in-built self-sabotage that acts as our automatic pilot!** You may not like your "home-made movie," but you've been stuck with it and you keep replaying it and experiencing the pain of self-sabotage, the pain of limiting beliefs and selling yourself short.

This is a critical point that you need to be aware of. What I need to repeat is that **there are 2 creations in life**. We follow **mental** creations (i.e., videos, DVDs or home movies) in our life that **physically** take us places in terms of who we are and how we behave and perform.

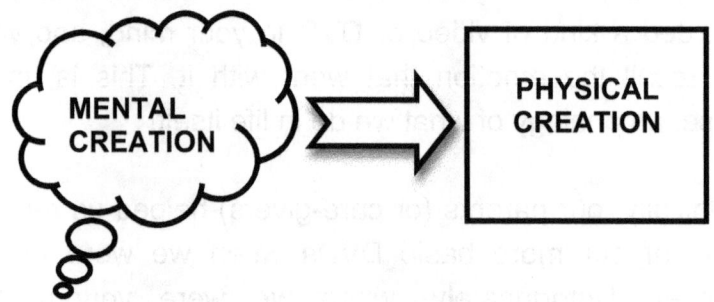

We record our DVDs, and they naturally or automatically play out the drama and scenes in our lives.

What happens though, if we have an actual video or DVD at home, for instance, and we don't like it anymore, or we want to get rid of it, or we're tired of watching it?

Answer: We erase it or tape over it or edit it.

In our own lives, these movies may have been influenced by others (like parents), but we arranged, directed and produced them ourselves. The good news though, is that we are still in control of the editing process even now. Hence, we do not have to keep viewing or looking at these horrid movies. We can, in fact, make our own changes and edits. Great news indeed!

To alter these old movies or videos and instead, create more powerful and positive DVDs which can come on automatically and naturally, is the pathway to the personal strength, purpose and energy in life that we desire.

So, how do we do it? We want to make sure that these new videos or DVDs are good, powerful movies. In Chapter 10, we will explore how to re-imagine, re-record and re-program ourselves.

Chapter 9 Summary

Like trying to do a jigsaw puzzle without the box with the picture on it, we can't achieve our goals without actually visualizing them.

Our mental picture determines our physical reality. Unfortunately, many of us have been captive to the early videos or home-made movies that we made up in our own minds and that we now keep playing and replaying automatically. These so-called movies in our minds keep us caught in the game of self-sabotage.

However, adopting the right mental picture can cause the impossible to happen. It can turn our lives around and put us on a new pathway.

CHAPTER 10

POSITIVE SELF-PICTURES

Re-Imagine Yourself

In 1960, a plastic-surgeon-turned-amateur-psychologist, Dr. Maxwell Maltz, wrote and had published, a book that would take off, achieve blockbuster best-seller status, and revolutionize the entire field of self-improvement.

His book, *PsychoCybernetics*, went on to reach over thirty million people and lives on today, even long after his death. Dr. Maltz came forward with the reason why so many people earnestly attempt to improve their lives with positive thinking alone, but never seem to get anywhere.

This is it in a nut-shell: **It is the *self-image* that governs what a person "can" and "can't" do**.

This explains, for example, why sincere, earnest dieters cannot stick to a weight loss program, why New Year's resolutions are never kept, why people procrastinate, and much, much more!

So, for example, if deep down inside the self-image, a person sees himself as athletically impaired, clumsy, the last kid ever to get picked to play a game, he can take golf lessons, watch golf videos, use golf gadgets, and learn the technical aspects of a good golf swing, but his actual game will automatically "snap back" to conform to the entrenched, natural images that he has of himself, of never being able to play sports properly.

As a way of changing the images and beliefs embedded in the *subconscious*, Maltz went on to develop unique "mental training exercises" to identify what is a person's self-image, and to modify it as he or she chooses.

"The mind will not reach toward achievement until it has clear objectives. The magic begins when we set goals. It is then that the switch is turned on, the current begins to flow, and the power to accomplish becomes a reality."

Author unknown

These mental training exercises have been used and endorsed by famous Olympic and professional athletes, sportsmen and sportswomen, authors, entertainment personalities, business leaders and others.

They are used today by countless people in all walks of life. **It is about creating positive self-pictures.** These pictures are at the heart of self-image.

Positive Self-Pictures and Imagery

Positive self-pictures or mental imagery is an exercise requiring conscious effort, but it is a way to influence the subconscious mind.

Subconscious expectations and internal dialogues are powerful influences on our perception of reality, our emotions and behaviors. Much of what exists in our subconscious was "recorded" in early life and can be thought of as a "psychological program" or a "script."

Techniques to change both THINKING and FEELING patterns to help you become a different person are explained below. You will learn to design a "psychological program" which will help support your conscious efforts including your silent self-talk and your spoken word which we have already covered in previous chapters.

Reprogramming Yourself

Much of our original psychological programming has been with us from childhood as we've already seen and prompts our negative attitudes and behaviors. If this programming is not to your liking because it is limiting or negative, then, no doubt, you would want to re-program it. You would want a new script.

With your CDs or DVDs, you can simply record over them if you wish or delete. With your computer, what you do if you don't want a particular file is to either edit it or delete it. A computer though, does not have to unlearn old habits. With people, new programming must be done gradually and the new "program" must be "run" numerous times before things become automatic. But, *it can be done!*

EXERCISE 10.1:

We need to erase our old pictures, or DVDs, and tape over them and edit them. Before we edit over our old DVDs, we need to work out what to put into our new DVD? How do you make the new DVD? How do you create a different picture for yourself that is much more positive?

You re-record yourself.

STEP 1: Identify what you want to re-record.

Review your life and identify those things which you would like to change, or the areas in which you would like to be better. What are the areas in which you'd like to improve?

If necessary, keep a journal for a day, a week or more in which you record your thoughts, your internal dialogue, your feelings and your behaviors. Record where you let yourself down, where you didn't show courage, where you backed off, where you said or did things that you regretted, where you felt badly.

If you like, review your Thoughts Record Sheets that you already filled out in Step 3 and 4 of the process for turning around negative thoughts from Chapter 5. Study them, and they will reveal a number of old "programming messages" that you can change or improve upon. But probably though, you already know your areas of self-sabotage.

Now, work out how you would really like to be. Instead of the ways in which you self-sabotage and you limit yourself, how would you really like to be (e.g., confident, happy, more loving, assertive, more friendly, more organized, more disciplined, more courageous, more independent, more social, a better listener, a better communicator, a good public speaker etc.)?

List your wants and how you'd like to be:

....

....

....

....

....

....

STEP 2: Write out a new script.

Write out new statements which will counteract old behaviors.

Start with "I am..." and make it positively worded. These statements must be written in **simple, active** and **positive** form. If they are complex, passive or negative, you will not get good results. Start with 1 to 4 reprogramming statements.

"**I am** ....

....

....

"**I am** ....

....

....

....

"I am ....

....

....

....

Now transfer each statement to a 3 x 5 index card (or something like that). This size card is handy to carry with you in a pocket, purse or briefcase.

"I am a loving person and I enjoy giving affection to my family and friends, and I enjoy receiving it as well."	"I am a confident person who enjoys interacting with others, and they enjoy interacting with me."

STEP 3: Daily – relax.

Find a relaxing place or position.

To use the reprogramming cards most effectively, you should be relaxed. To achieve deep relaxation you can sit in a hot bath, sit or lie down, or meditate. Perhaps put on some music to help you relax. Just spend a few minutes first relaxing.

STEP 4: Imagine – fantasize – visualize.

Once relaxed, read each card aloud several times -- hear the words, believe them, let them sink into your relaxed mind. Then **imagine, daydream, or fantasize** doing what's on the card as though you're watching a home video or looking at photos of yourself. These do not have to be Hollywood-type movies, but instead, can be snap-shots of yourself.

Most importantly, as you see the pictures in your head, **feel the emotion,** and live it. This is critical in that you need to not only see yourself in your mind's eye being successful, but you need to really feel the emotion that goes along with it.

STEP 5: Do this for about 2 minutes per card.

Inserting images into your conscious, but highly relaxed mind will help you open your *subconscious* mind. You must "reprogram" your subconscious before it can support your new objectives.

Read your cards *daily* (or twice daily, morning and night, if you like) for several months, and visualize yourself in order to condition your mind until the scenarios on your cards become "second nature" if you like.

You can read your cards anytime for additional reinforcement, but using the reprogramming routine before sleep is particularly powerful, because your subconscious is active periodically during sleep (that's why we dream). Your subconscious will absorb what your conscious mind visualized before sleep if you use the routine regularly.

To review, the simple steps to reprogram yourself include:

- **Write simple, active, positive statements that you want to record (one per card).**

- **Achieve a state of deep relaxation. Sit or lie down.**

- **Read each statement aloud several times.**

- **Visualize and imagine doing what's on the card.**

- **Feel the emotion!**

- **If you do this before you go to sleep, then let your subconscious absorbs the ideas (if you do these exercises at night).**

- **Do this daily – this is critical!**

- **Continue this for a minimum of 21 days as a trial (many people do this until it becomes absolutely entrenched in their minds over a few months).**

This is recommended as a daily exercise for the entire length of your life.

Every day. These pictures are critical to your mental survival and good health. You may not continue to use the same cards, since over a period of time your pictures can become second nature and entrenched, and your behavior and attitudes therefore change as you planned. Therefore, feel free to create some other cards (and pictures) as necessary.

You will feel the results starting to kick in after about 3 weeks – remember, "Rome wasn't built in a day" – stick with it; the results are powerful.

Do it every day. For the rest of your life!

Get into the habit of doing it – just like you get into the habit of eating, sleeping, dressing and so on.

Chapter 10 Summary

Mental training exercises can be used to re-record our mental pictures from those that feature our insecurities to those that feature the great things we can do with our lives and for ourselves.

An exercise is introduced and outlined to help us re-record and introduce positive images to our subconscious mind. This is important to undertake since the subconscious acts as our automatic pilot and we want to ensure that our pictures are naturally positive and enhancing rather than the other way round.

"We do not see with our eyes, we see with our brains."

Dr. John Medina

CHAPTER 11

DISCIPLINE

A "Dirty" Word

How do we really make all this happen, though? It occurs through that word that many people believe is a "dirty word," i.e., discipline.

Remember that I said that there were no short-cuts. It is DISCIPLINE that is required if you really want to change your self-sabotage, eliminate your fears, get rid of your limiting beliefs and feel success.

"Discipline is the bridge between goals and accomplishments."

Jim Rohn

Going to the gym to get fit and lose weight just once won't be enough! One trip to the gym won't do it.

The discipline of incorporating these basic exercises into your daily routine is critical to your success.

The discipline of...

> ...keeping track of your thoughts each day and then spending 10 minutes each night filling out your **Thoughts Record Sheet**.

The discipline of...

> ...spending up to 10 minutes a day **saying your statements out loud** with feeling and intensity.

The discipline of...

> ...**visualizing your positive pictures** each day for 2 minutes per card.

Discipline will allow you to reach toward your full potential. To be the kind of person you were destined to be.

It is a truism that the majority of the population "know" how to do things, whatever those "things" are, but the same majority do NOT "do" them. Sure they talk about them. They might, in fact, plan to do them. But they do not actually end up doing them. It's called the Knowing-Doing gap.

> *"Life rewards action, not good intentions."*
>
> Darryl Cross

I have been impressed with the urgency of doing. Knowing is not enough; we must apply. Being willing is not enough; we must do. Knowing is not enough. Being willing is not enough. You must do.

What is the definition of "stupidity?" **Answer:** Doing the same thing you did yesterday and expecting a different result. Don't fall into that trap. Do it differently.

> *"If you do what you've always done,
> you'll get what you've always got."*
>
> — Author unknown

You have a responsibility to yourself and those around you to be the best that you can be. It is your gift to yourself to fulfill your potential and to be the best that you can be.

> *"If you want to be something different –
> you have to do something different."*
>
> — Author unknown

Obstacles

We now have **three powerful strategies** to turn your life around and to start to feel more confident. See Figure 11.1 on the next page.

1. Monitoring your **self-talk** by using the Thoughts Record Sheet (see the Appendix).

2. Saying **positive statements out loud** so your brain "gets it."

3. Using positive visualizations to **create a positive self-picture**.

Figure 11.1 The 3 Main Strategies for Stopping Self-Sabotage

Conscious:

- **Your Silent Self-Talk**
  - use your Thoughts Sheet
- **Your Spoken Word**
  - practice your positive talking out loud

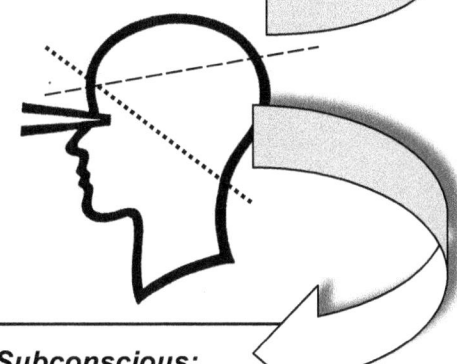

Subconscious:

- **Your Self-Picture (DVDs, pictures, 'home-movies')**
  - automatically come on
  - act as your automatic pilot
  - work out what you really want
  - re-record a new movie
  - visualize daily and feel the emotion

What would it take for you to instigate these strategies? ***What will you do as a result of reading this book? What will you do now?***

For some of you, there will be no issue. You see the need. You have felt the pain of letting yourself down. Alternatively, you have felt the sense of feeling proud and you want to create that feeling again for yourself. You can see what improving your self-confidence is going to mean for your life, your relationships, your career, yourself. You will go ahead and put these strategies into place...and you'll reap the rewards.

Others of you will continue to sabotage yourselves. You may think that these strategies are a good idea. You may think that they make good sense. You may have liked what you read. But somehow or other, you won't do it.

"The difference between a successful person and others is not strength, not a lack of knowledge, but rather a lack of will."

Vince Lombardi

The time investment is about 10 minutes per day to fill out your Thoughts Record Sheet (see the Appendix); 10 minutes per day to say your statements out-loud; and about 6 minutes per day for your positive visualizations. That's about 26 minutes. Not a bad investment when the results can be life-changing.

So, let me ask you – **What would get in the way of you doing these exercises?** If you don't want to do all of the exercises, maybe you can do just one. Maybe just start with one. What would stop you? What would get in the way? Be honest with yourself.

Would it be that you can't be bothered? Too busy? Procrastinate? Put it off? Think it's corny? Don't believe that it will work? Can't find the time? Too much like hard work?

EXERCISE 11.1:

Be honest and list below what would get in the way of you completing these exercises:

Obstacle 1: ....

....

....

....

....

Obstacle 2: ....

....

....

....

....

Obstacle 3: ....

....

....

....

....

Obstacle 4: ....

....

....

....

....

So, how can you overcome these obstacles? What would you have to do to get around these issues or problems? Write down below what you'd need to do to get around the issue.

EXERCISE 11.2:

Get around obstacle 1 by: ....
....
....
....

Get around obstacle 2 by: ....
....
....
....

Get around obstacle 3 by: ....
....
....
....

Get around obstacle 4 by: ....
....
....
....

> *"You cannot change your destination overnight, but you can change your direction overnight."*
>
> Jim Rohn

Make it Happen

How prepared are you to do this now?

Are you going to be true to yourself?

Will you give yourself, say, a 10-day trial on this?

Perhaps try out one of the strategies outlined in the previous chapters (or perhaps 2 strategies, or all 3) for 10 days.

One last exercise. Are you up for one final task?

EXERCISE 11.3:

Recall a person in your life who had a profound positive impact on you. This person does not have to be your parent, it can be anyone in your life. It can be a past teacher at school, a friend, an aunt or uncle, a business partner, a boss, a trainer, a sports coach, a grandparent – it can be anyone. It could be someone who is still alive or someone who has passed on. **Who was/is this person?** (Write down their name.)

....

Now answer the following:

- ✓ **What did they do?**
- ✓ **What did they do that you liked?**
- ✓ **How did you feel about yourself when you were with them?**

....
....
....
....
....
....

As you look at your responses, what did this person really do for you? They may have done a number of things. When I ask this question in my workshops, I get responses like, they "listened to me," "encouraged me," "supported me," "challenged me," "made me feel important," and "made me feel special." Ultimately, I think you'll find that they helped you **to believe in yourself.**

These people believed in you, and allowed you to believe in yourself. In who they were, and how they communicated with you, and how they supported you, they allowed you to believe in yourself.

> *"The future depends on what we do in the present."*
>
> Mahatma Gandhi

Now it's your turn to believe in yourself for you. Do it for your future. Do it for you. These other people believed in you. They had faith in you. Do it because you don't want to live a life of regrets. Do it because it's your real purpose in life to be your full self, your whole self. It's what you were created for. You're worth it. You deserve it.

**Practice makes perfect.
Repetition is the mother of skill.**

> *"Successful people are ordinary people that consistently do the hard things that most ordinary people think too hard."*
>
> Steve Hunter

"Great things are not done by impulse but by a series of small things brought together."

Vincent van Gogh

"Life is like riding a bicycle – you don't fall off unless you stop pedaling."

Claude Pepper

Step out and do something different for yourself.

Eliminate obstacles and make it happen. Just do it.

I wish you well on your inner journey.

Chapter 11 Summary

Discipline is the 'dirty' word that we must learn to love in order to make these exercises work. There are no shortcuts.

There are three major strategies that underpin who you are as a person and how you present; two strategies for the conscious mind and one for the subconscious mind. Exercises have been outlined for you for each arena.

You can do **all** three exercises with an investment of around 26 minutes a day – well worth it for what you are going to accomplish.

What's stopping you doing these exercises? By writing down how you plan to overcome the obstacles to success, you can conquer them because you expose them.

Believe in yourself, and you can do it. You're worth it.

APPENDIX

THOUGHTS RECORD SHEETS
A BLANK ONE AND A COMPLETED SAMPLE

THOUGHTS RECORD SHEET

DATE & TIME	WHERE	NEGATIVE EMOTIONS (Intensity 1-10)	TRIGGERING EVENT	NEGATIVE THOUGHTS	RATIONAL THOUGHTS	RATE EMOTION AGAIN

Permission granted to photocopy for personal use
handouts/thoughts sheet1.doc

Crossways Consulting

Appendix

THOUGHTS RECORD SHEET   SAMPLE

DATE & TIME	WHERE	NEGATIVE EMOTIONS (Intensity 1-10)	TRIGGERING EVENT	NEGATIVE THOUGHTS	RATIONAL THOUGHTS	RATE EMOTION AGAIN
14/6 8.40	School yard	Anxious (7)	Another parent walked past me & didn't say hello.	"What have I done?" "Why did he ignore me?" "Have I upset him somehow?"	"There's no evidence to suggest that I have upset him. Maybe he just didn't see me. Maybe he was pre-occupied. I can't do anything about it now so I'll wait until next time & ask him then."	Anxious (2)
15/6 3.30 p.m.	Work	Depressed-Down (6)	Computer crashed & I lost all my work.	"This always happens to me! Bad stuff always happens to me. Why me? Why now?"	"'Stuff' happens to every one of us some stage. Sure it's inconvenient & unpleasant, but it's not the end of the world. I can cope with this."	Depressed-Down (2)
16/6 5.45 pm	Home	Guilty (6)	Received a letter from a friend who was recently married	"I should have gone to her wedding."	"It was inconvenient at the time. Besides, she wouldn't be writing to me if she felt ticked off or annoyed at me."	Guilty (1)

Permission granted to photocopy for personal use

Crossways Consulting

SAMPLE

133

ABOUT THE AUTHOR

Dr. Darryl Cross, PhD
Leadership / Careers Coach & Psychologist

Fellow, Australian Psychological Society
Fellow, Australian Institute of Management
Certified Personal & Executive Coach, College of Executive Coaching
Professional Certified Coach, International Coach Federation
Member, National Speakers Association
Accredited Facilitator, Mindshop Australia Ltd
Foreign Affiliate, American Psychological Association
Registered Psychologist

> **Darryl assists people to maximize their potential and reach their goals.**

Dr. Darryl Cross is a leadership and personal coach as well as a clinical and organizational psychologist. He is an author, international speaker and university lecturer.

As a **Leadership Coach**, for **executives and senior managers**, this might mean a focus on effective leadership, dealing with difficult staff, increasing productivity and succession planning. He has over 2000 hours of coaching having been a coach now for over 10 years.

For those with **business concerns**, it might mean work-life balance, career progression, job dissatisfaction or dealing with conflict.

For those with **personal concerns**, it may include addressing a lack of career direction, lack of confidence or relational issues.

Having gone through the discipline of tertiary study, he completed his Psychology Honors Degree in Psychology at Flinders University, South Australia. He gained his Doctorate in Psychology from the University of Queensland.

In 2001, Darryl completed a Professional Development Certificate in Coaching Practice through the

Department of Psychology at the University of Sydney. More recently, he completed graduate studies in coaching with the College of Executive Coaching in California, USA. He is now a **Professional Certified Coach** with the International Coach Federation.

As a **university lecturer**, he tutored and lectured in psychology at the University of Queensland in Brisbane for seven years and lectured at Macquarie University in Sydney, New South Wales for two years. He is now a sessional lecturer in "Leadership Dynamics" for the MBA program at the International Graduate School of Business for the University of South Australia, and lectures in the Department of Psychology Doctoral Program.

He **knows how organizations work** from his first appointment for three years as an occupational psychologist with the Australian government, and from when he was appointed as director of a unit at the Adelaide Children's Hospital. He held that position until moving into his own business. He has also acted as a **management consultant** to a range of companies and government departments and has conducted attitude and stress surveys.

Darryl Cross has been **training and speaking** for almost three decades at a variety of keynotes and workshops for business, professional and non-professional groups on topics ranging from "Stress Management", "Coping with Change", "Handling the

Angry Customer", "Career Progression" to "Managers As Coaches."

As an **author**, Darryl has published numerous papers for national and overseas academic journals as well as the popular press. He has also written a book on raising adolescents, one on parenting children, a book on depression in the workplace, one for business leaders on the power of listening, as well as a book on managing Gen X and Gen Y. He has also authored a career guidance test called the "Vocational Interest Questionnaire", which is available online for both adolescents and adults.

Academic training in psychology and specific training in coaching, together with life experience, means that Darryl has come up with practical ways to use life principles that work. He has a knack of being able to say it all simply.

www.DrDarryl.com
www.FindACareerPath.com
www.viq.com.au
www.TeenagerTroubleShooting.com
www.GrowingUpChildren.com

Crossways Consulting
PO Box 2000
North Adelaide
South Australia
Australia 5006

enquiries@crossways.com.au

www.ingramcontent.com/pod-product-compliance
Lightning Source LLC
Chambersburg PA
CBHW071437160426
43195CB00013B/1943